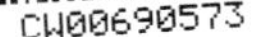

Featherings

Featherings

True Stories in Search of Birds

EDITED BY
Vernon RL Head

All author royalties will be donated to the FitzPatrick Institute of African Ornithology to support ongoing ornithological research.

First published by Jacana Media (Pty) Ltd in 2017

10 Orange Street
Sunnyside
Auckland Park 2092
South Africa
+2711 628 3200
www.jacana.co.za

ISBN 978-1-4314-2579-2

Cover design by publicide
Set in MrsEaves 11.5/15pt
Printed and bound by CTP Printers, Cape Town

See a complete list of Jacana titles at www.jacana.co.za

Contents

Preface

Watching wild birds upon the land, inside a cloud or deep within an ocean is to see differently. There is something about the movement of these creatures that connects us to a primordial past of answers. Such is the language of feathers.

And it is this way of seeing that proffers stories coming from birds, each one made and told in glorious diversity of thought, each one an instruction, a message or an idea, like the new songs trees make every time the wind moves between leaves.

In our frenetic world of walls – the high borders of sovereignty and greed; the low boundaries of misunderstanding and misguided aspirations – are to be found the freedoms that come on wings beyond walls.

This very personal collection of tales is important: an offering of moments in Nature that we hope will inspire contemplation. Perhaps it is time to slow down for a minute, searching for a pause in the day, time to listen … time to look.

– Vernon RL Head
June 2017

When heavens fall

By David Allan

It was the unique song given from its high, hunting display flight that gave the game away. I knew I'd certainly never heard it before and strongly suspected that it might be what we were after. Warwick Tarboton, for whom I worked at the time, arrived a few days later and I took him out to the site east of the small Highveld hamlet of Amersfoort and he confirmed the bird as Rudd's Lark. This was in the early 1980s and long before the days of the 'apps' that you'd use now to solve such conundrums. Indeed, it was just before the advent of decent bird field guides and commercial bird-call cassette tapes, never mind cellphones and their associated wizardry. Guy Gibbon was one of the first of the subsequent visitors to come and share in the find. What sorcery it is that I can today still play the magic of that first bird's call on my Roberts smartphone app from Guy's recording taken all those decades ago.

Another visitor was the rambunctious Ian Sinclair who, from a perch on the bonnet of my bakkie while we drove down the rutted track, spotted a bird furtively flush from the grassland. Leaping to the ground he instantaneously pinpointed a well-concealed nest with three eggs. This was a landmark find. The only previous known nest had been discovered by the legendary Austin Roberts 70 years earlier in 1913 at Wakkerstroom about 45 km to the south. In his account of the species, Roberts provided perhaps one of the most evocative, and yet least useful, descriptions of a bird's call when he likened the song to 'a person whistling with bubbles in the mouth'. My take on the song was a little different. Fiddling around with a clunky sonogram machine at Wits University (another thing you do wholly digitally these days) I was able to see that this lark achieves the endless variety to its songs by intermittently cycling the elements used to compose them from a larger repertoire, coupled with shifting the order of presentation of these elements. The result is an ever-changing song-sheet aimed presumably at retaining the attention of the listener. But the real mystery is that although each Rudd's Lark composition sounds quite different to all others, it is still immediately identifiable as belonging to the species.

Ian's treasure came during a particularly purple patch related to nesting larks at that time. Warwick, Garth Batchelor and I had over the previous two months discovered 11 nests of the equally enigmatic Botha's Lark in the Amersfoort area. Garth had spurred this initiative when he located the first nest in mid-November. These were the first ever known breeding records for that species and the focused effort the three of us put into making this breakthrough, subsequently published in the journal *Ostrich*, will forever rank high in my birding memories.

I was to go on to encounter Rudd's Lark at several other localities in the Highveld of the then eastern Transvaal (now Mpumalanga province), typically on isolated higher-lying plateaus and often around moist depressions at these sites. I also came across many additional nests but repeat visits to these soon suggested that such human disturbance tended to result in breeding failure. My Rudd's Lark adventures played a role in influencing the direction of my life. A team from the FitzPatrick Institute that included Phil Hockey and Richard Dean came up to do more detailed investigations of Rudd's Lark habitat and I dutifully took them on a tour of my localities for the species. Not long afterwards, this interaction resulted in my departing the Highveld and re-locating to Cape Town to work at the Institute on bustards and cranes in the west of the country – where I was also to become acquainted for the first time with the many other species of intriguing larks inhabiting those fascinating landscapes.

A few years later found me at the then Avian Demography Unit at UCT working on the first Southern African Bird Atlas Project and my final meaningful liaison with Rudd's Lark. While doing fieldwork for the atlas in a far-flung corner of Transkei above Ncora Dam I suddenly heard the unmistakable song of my long-lost friend. It was a single bird displaying in a small patch of suitable habitat in an otherwise hopelessly over-grazed environment. This record was in some ways even more significant than my earlier finds as it was some 200 km south of the previously known southern limit of the species, which comprised the isolated Matatiele population in East Griqualand. I could not tarry long but Carl Vernon subsequently travelled up from East London and re-located the bird at the locality, proving it to be more than a one-day wonder. A little later in 1996, two small outliers of the species were also found by local birder Sandy Stretton in the Molteno area almost as far south.

The Matatiele population was first discovered in about 1910 by Claude Finch-Davies, the renowned bird artist whose latter career was tragically besmirched by scandal when he was caught damaging books in the library of the then Transvaal (now Ditsong) Museum in obsessive pursuit of his artistic endeavours. The Rudd's Lark findings of both Finch-Davies and Roberts came very close after the very first discovery of the species by the British ornithologist Claude Grant at Wakkerstroom in 1904 during a wide-ranging expedition funded by the mining magnate Charles Rudd.

The few occasions that I've come across Rudd's Lark subsequently have all been at the well-worn Wakkerstroom sites. Otherwise I'm reliant on hearing news second-hand. And that news on balance does not sound good for this South African endemic with a frighteningly restricted distribution. Although still found regularly at isolated sites in a fragmented range along the escarpment between Amersfoort in the north and Verkykerskop (the latter in the Free State) to the south, the species has apparently disappeared from many of its old 'Transvaal' Highveld haunts, including all those to the north of Amersfoort. The celebrated Matatiele population, where the birds once occurred more densely on the ground than anywhere else, has evidently completely vanished. Recent searches at Ncora Dam have come up empty-handed, although the species persists in the Molteno area.

There's a saying that the only positive outcome in having the heavens fall is that we may then catch larks. But of course the reality is quite different. When the heavens fall, everything, including larks and men, will fall with it.

Sandgrouse – special denizens of deserts

By Mark D. Anderson

I PREFER DESERTS TO FORESTS. I always have, and always will. I am more at home among the mesas and buttes of the Karoo and the rolling red dunes of the Kalahari. It is the wide-open spaces, the endless vistas, the clear skies, and the harshness of these dry environments that appeal to me. I am also fascinated by the animals and plants that are superbly adapted to survive in these seemingly inhospitable places.

The Kalahari and Karoo birds have fascinated me for many years. As the provincial nature conservation ornithologist in the Northern Cape it was my responsibility to study them, to monitor their numbers, and to implement actions to conserve them. Initially it was important for me to get to know these birds. I took pleasure in learning to identify non-descript larks, understanding the nomadic movements of sandgrouse and bustards, and studying and determining mitigation measures to address the many threats affecting endangered eagles and vultures.

One group of birds that I got to know intimately were sandgrouse, and three species occur in the Northern Cape. These fascinating birds, which are closely related to waders, are, as with so many of our country's birds, facing many anthropogenic threats. The beautiful Namaqua Sandgrouse, found only in the arid parts of South Africa and Namibia, falls victim to wingshooters' shotguns, flies into overhead telephone and electricity cables, and its eggs and nestlings are bearing the brunt of significantly larger populations of terrestrial predators, such as mongooses and snakes, in its core breeding range, in Bushmanland.

One of my most memorable birding experiences was a morning spent with sandgrouse at a pan located near the Skurweberg, a small and isolated quartzite mountain located at the south-western edge of the magnificent Kalahari Desert.

Starting off early from the white and sometimes roaring sands of Witsand, we headed off to the pan. Our group consisted of my wife, Tania, our five-year-old son, Ryan, the eccentric and late Professor Steven Piper, and well known botanist and lepidopterist, Christopher Willis.

We had heard from Penn Lloyd, who was studying Namaqua Sandgrouse for his PhD, that as many as 20 000 sandgrouse were drinking at this pan. That was a sight we had to see. We arrived at the pan at about 08:30, two hours after sunrise, and shortly before the first sandgrouse were expected to arrive. We decided that our viewing place would be on the eastern side of the pan, so that we would have the sun at our backs. We concealed ourselves among some quartzite rocks, and black thorn and three-thorn bushes.

We sat quietly, breathing in the crisp air and savouring the silence. The quietness was occasionally interrupted by the calls of Fawn-coloured Larks, Ant-eating Chats and a distant Pale Chanting Goshawk sitting on a camelthorn tree. We waited patiently, wondering what to expect.

We turned to each other and smiled, as the characteristic 'kelkiewyn' calls of Namaqua Sandgrouse could be heard in the distance. Individual sandgrouse and small flocks started to arrive. They landed a short distance from the water, and then, when they felt safe, cautiously hurried to the edge of the pan to drink. After taking a few quick sips, they left as quickly as they had arrived. Some birds were more nervous, and these circled the pan several times before picking up the courage to land. Now, about 15 minutes after the first sandgrouse arrived, there were many more birds, perhaps many hundreds. We sat quietly, spellbound by what we were witnessing. The sky was filled with flying sandgrouse, and the stillness of this quiet place was replaced with a magnificent cacophony of bird calls.

Listening carefully, we picked up another call: the 'glug-glug' call of the Burchell's Sandgrouse. This species usually arrives a bit later than its Namaqua cousin. Their numbers also steadily increased, and soon we estimated that we were watching several thousand individuals of both species of sandgrouse. Steven whispered to me that we were witnessing one of the world's most significant bird spectacles, and I nodded in agreement.

Looking through our binoculars, we noticed that the Burchell's Sandgrouse were behaving differently. Some of the male birds also walked into the water, wetting their belly feathers. This indicated that the birds were breeding, and what they were doing was saturating their specially designed feathers with water. They would then fly back to their nest, up to 60 km away, and allow their nestlings to sip the life-giving water from their belly feathers. We marvelled at this amazing adaptation.

About an hour after the first sandgrouse arrived, the number of birds was far fewer. And a few minutes later, they were all gone! The air was eerily quiet. Within the space of a little more than 60 minutes some 20 000 sandgrouse had descended on this small pan.

We were extremely privileged to witness this natural wonder, something that all keen birdwatchers should attempt to do at least once in their lifetime. Until today, whenever I see a sandgrouse, I think back to this special spring morning in the Kalahari.

The birds our teachers

By Mark Brown

Cramp had started setting in... Sweat was dripping, limbs frozen... For fifteen minutes now, the most powerful raptor in Africa and I had been eye-balling each other... This was seriously stressful stuff! Would the plan work? Would we be able to outsmart this magnificent bird or would we end up wasting our time? Another ten minutes ticked by... My hands were stiff from holding the camera in one set position. Apart from blinking, and breathing, we hadn't moved... Then, deciding we were safe, the bird dropped down onto the ground, a mere ten metres away from us! Right next to our trap! After a few more stressful minutes, contemplating whether this supposedly easy meal was worth the effort or not, it made a dash, and we had it! With Kiwi-born Shane McPherson holding it, and all of us shaking from adrenalin-induced excitement, we were able to ring and measure this immature African Crowned Eagle, the first one trapped as part of Shane's MSc on the species. What a moment! Being up close and personal with such an immense creature, within centimetres of talons that rip open prey several times its size, this was undoubtedly one of those experiences that made me grateful to be alive. Over the next few years, Shane went on to get not only his MSc, but also his PhD studying these majestic birds. There are now probably close to a hundred individuals carrying our rings in the Greater Durban, Pietermaritzburg and KZN South Coast region, giving us regular insight into their movements as they are seen around these built-up areas.

For me, birding is so much more than just seeing and enjoying a species. Being an ornithologist and a citizen scientist has enabled me to delve deeper into the mysterious and marvellous world of birds, in ways I never dreamed of before. Whether it be by trapping and ringing a species, setting up cameras at nests to study behaviour and diet, tracking birds with GPS units, monitoring breeding attempts, conducting CWAC counts or even just good action-packed atlasing, there is *always* something new to experience and to learn about our feathered friends.

Apart from nectar-feeding birds and raptors, my favourite groups to study must be shorebirds and seabirds. Holding an African Black Oystercatcher in your hand, or re-sighting a 20-year-old bird, breeding on the beach I walk on near home, is just marvellous. Working on islands, where seabirds have no fear of man (having never co-evolved with mammalian predators), is the weirdest thing out. Walking up to an incubating White-tailed Tropicbird, picking it up off the nest, ringing it and putting it back with no fuss just doesn't seem natural. Working with Dr Lorinda Hart on tropicbirds, noddies and terns has led to some interesting discoveries. For instance, did you know tropicbirds incubate their eggs with their *feet*? We used a thermal imaging camera to show this unusual pattern of breeding. Birds are just so cool!

Birding to me is also about people, the joy and emotions of sharing experiences around birds. So many of my birding memories are actually intertwined with memories of people. Birding crosses boundaries – cultural, demographic and geographical ones. It takes you places you might never go. For instance, what's the one place birders will always look for when in a new town, that everyone else avoids? That's right – the sewerage works! For over ten years I had the privilege of organising monthly ringing sessions at Darvill Bird Sanctuary in Pietermaritzburg, South Africa's longest running ringing station (35 years and counting!). Many a day was spent by a diverse team of people heading out before dawn, as early as 4 am in summer, to set up the nets to see what we would catch. With a rich aroma of, well, you know ... wafting around us constantly, every outing was a buzz, filled with fun, food, knowledge gained and great birds. Shernice Soobramooney was the real hero – driving out every month from Durban (so leaving over an hour earlier than us locals), and always arriving with a bag full of Woolworths goodies – chips, cakes, koeksisters, brownies, you name it! Meyrick Bowker was the wise old timer who had participated at the station for 20 years, training multiple generations of young passionate ornithologists-to-be. Birding is actually always about people. Somewhere, someone got each of us interested in birds, and mentored us into the hobby. For me, Prof. Gordon Maclean was an early inspiration, and Prof. Colleen Downs a magnificent mentor, encouraging me and challenging me to get to where I am today, as a conservationist and as a birder – just don't go walking through forests with her looking for parrots – you may never come out!

In fact, training young passionate conservationists is probably the part of birding I get the biggest kick out of myself. I have had the privilege of working closely with over 50 passionate young up-and-coming conservationists from all over the world in the last 15 years, and have so many special memories of experiencing birding through new eyes – each time one of them got hooked, it was like starting afresh all over again. From training someone to trap and hold a raptor, find a shorebird nest, extract a bird from a mistnet, conduct a point count or identify difficult groups of birds, through to the more mundane parts of being a conservation scientist – setting up adequate research protocols, designing projects, managing data, using statistics, writing papers, raising funds, managing teams, applying for permits – it all comes with great memories of spending time in the field, sighting a trogon for the first time, netting an oooh aaah bird, as the late Prof. Steven Piper would say (like a Malachite Kingfisher for instance) or recording a species out of range – special times with special people.

Children just ooze passion for birding, and soak up close encounters with birds like a sponge. Being able to expose young South Africans to the joys of birds, through organised outings, is another of my favourite activities. A few vivid memories stick out – hosting 95 people for a bird-ringing session in the Fynbos, and not catching a single bird for the first hour and a half – yet making up for it with just three birds in the hand – a Cape White-eye, a Southern Double-collared Sunbird and a Willow Warbler. Sharing the knowledge gained from studying these species for over 15 years, and seeing eyes get excited when you talk about the effects of climate change on white-eyes and how they cope really well with change (work done by Dr Lindy Thompson for her PhD with Prof. Downs and I), or about how a sunbird needs to drink *three* times it's body weight each day (that equates to a 50 kg person drinking 150 litres in a day!) or sharing the incredible story of a 12 g Willow Warbler flying to Siberia and back each year, is truly a special thing. Other great memories include releasing three rehabilitated raptors with a group of 65, also at a Fynbos ringing session. Auctioning off the right for kids to release two Forest Buzzards and an African Harrier Hawk had been a last-minute idea – but it worked! Not only did we raise important funds for raptor rehabilitation and conservation, but the looks on several young faces as they helped me release these magnificent birds back into the wild are engrained in my mind forever – and I am sure they are now passionate conservationists at heart!

It would be remiss of me not to mention one more important group of people that I bird with – my amazing family. I am blessed with a wife, Kelly, and two children, Jesse and Kate, who love birds almost as much as I do. Many a family holiday or weekend is spent ringing or atlasing together, and it is indeed a hobby for the whole family. The beauty of birding as a hobby is, of course, that it can be done everywhere! I have birded in the middle of large cities, at airports, in game reserves, on islands, in gardens and often frequently while driving – a dangerous component of birding that I am really surprised doesn't lead to more accidents!

In my mind, the question for all of us as birders is obvious – what are we as individuals doing to ensure birds are taken care of? Around the world, birds are being affected by man – there is now not a single place on the planet where we have not had a significant impact, and birds are often right up there on the list of groups that are impacted the most. Fortunately, there is also a global groundswell of work being done to tackle these impacts, and it is heartening to see so many dedicated birders getting involved in projects aimed at documenting first-hand how birds are responding to the Anthropocene, and also assisting professional conservationists to mitigate these effects. Working with passionate young conservationists leads me to boldly state that the future looks bright. What we still need is more of us, ordinary everyday birders, to throw our hats in the ring and get involved. I challenge us all to do so – start local by seeking out a BirdLife South Africa affiliated bird club, and get involved!

Congo Peacock journey

By Callan Cohen

A LARGE SHAPE MOVED in the dense undergrowth of the central African forest and I swung my eyes to the left.

It was December 2005 and I was hoping to see a Congo Peacock. For me, even just a glimpse would represent the revealing of one of wild Africa's most alluring secrets. No one I knew had ever seen one.

There is a painting of a male on the cover of one of the giant volumes of the scholarly *Birds of Africa*. That a bird of such large size and bright colours could elude centuries of scientific exploration is a testament both to the remoteness of the forest wilderness where it occurs and its extremely secretive nature. It was only in 1936, once almost all of Africa's birds and mammals were already well known to the world, that an American ornithologist drew the link between some mysterious feathers in a chief's head-dress from the Congo and some dusty specimens in the back room of a colonial museum. The mythical mbulu-bird was real, and the discovery of a wild species of peacock in Africa was a zoological sensation. It created such interest that local hunters were employed to trap a few birds that were brought to zoos in the northern hemisphere.

And yet, in the vast equatorial forests of the Congo basin, Africa's equivalent of the Amazon jungle, few outsiders had ever managed to see the bird in the wild. The Congo Peacock (also known as Congo Peafowl) is only known from the central and eastern Democratic Republic of the Congo, one of the world's last great wildernesses. Access to its range has long been limited by war and a lack of roads. There were only a few published records of encounters in the wild, mainly the occasional bird stumbled upon by dedicated primatologists and conservationists while walking hundreds of kilometres of transects through the forests in search of Bonobos (pygmy chimpanzees) and other mammals. When I discovered that I was going to be visiting my wife at a primate research camp in the heart of the Democratic Republic of Congo where she was working, I quickly checked the coordinates. The camp was within the expected distribution of Congo Peacock, and I would be based there for a month.

A childhood interest had by this point grown into a lifelong obsession to see and understand all of Africa's birds. The preceding years had found me exploring the remotest areas of the continent, both participating in ornithological expeditions and leading groups of dedicated birders for a specialist tour company I had founded while at university. Although I had never travelled to the Congo itself, I had recently birded large areas of lowland forest in adjacent Gabon, Cameroon and Uganda, and was already familiar with most of the species one could expect to find there. I'd also gained experience with recent searches for other extremely rare and secretive gamebirds that very few people in the world had ever seen. This included four days' trekking into the unspoiled central Tanzanian mountains to watch Udzungwa Forest Partridge for less than a second (success!), and, on a West African volcano, falling asleep overnight in a poacher's shelter to the stench of smoking meat for an early morning sighting of Mount Cameroon Francolin. Congo Peacock would not be easy to find but I had plenty of time to try. I was 20-something years old and full of confidence I would see it.

The tiny charter plane had taken off in the capital Kinshasa, initially rising over the Congo River – a volume of water so wide it seemed to stretch from horizon to horizon in the tropical haze. After bouncing eastwards for over two hours above ever-denser forest and snaking networks of interlinking river tributaries, with no roads and almost no signs of human habitation, we eventually landed with a bump and skidded to a halt on a small sandy airstrip. I tumbled out of the plane door, threw up behind some bushes and staggered back to the plane to help unpack bags of supplies. Before I even realised it, the plane was sweeping overhead again, the sound of the propellers eventually disappearing through layers of trees. It was a 30 km walk to the camp where my wife was based, which we needed to reach by nightfall. The small village beside the airstrip, an old mission station, was the last contact with any signs of people (besides passing the occasional hunter coming along the trail in the opposite direction, a monkey slung across his shoulder, frothy blood dribbling out of its lifeless mouth and tail looped around its head for ease of carrying). Initially the guides led me along a clear trail through the forest and occasional open areas; later the trees became taller and denser. Large areas were flooded and we waded waist-deep through the forest, stumbling over submerged tree buttresses. I didn't have a camera, so my main focus was to keep my trusty sound-recording equipment from getting ruined (documenting the sounds made by African birds was one of my major interests). Eventually we reached a large river and the final stretch was done in a dugout canoe. The small collection of dome tents and flimsy wooden structures in a cramped forest clearing was to be my base for the next month.

The moment I stepped into that clearing and reunited with my wife after months spent apart remains one of my most treasured memories. Some of the days would be spent with her, assisting and learning more about her Bonobo research (or keeping her company during her bouts of malaria), but there would also be many mornings for bird surveying and indulging my quest. The research assistants at the camp, once local hunters themselves, were small in stature and had a wealth of knowledge and tales surrounding the forest. They confirmed Congo Peacock was in the area, but hadn't seen any recently, and despite spending their entire lives hunting in the forest, it turned out they had only seen the birds a handful of times. They laughed among themselves when they wished me luck. The next day I was in the forest.

The large shape in my peripheral vision had disappeared. I stood almost completely still for about five minutes, waiting for my heart beat to slow down, and hoping it might reveal itself again. Nothing happened, so I crept slowly deeper into the forest, carefully scanning the gaps among the leaves for any signs of movement. Nothing. I was just turning back towards the trail when I glanced down at my feet: overturned leaves and fresh scrapings in the damp leaf-litter. I had pored over all the old literature related to Congo Peacock and this was one of the characteristic signs of their feeding that local hunters had described.

But I'd also seen similar scrapings from Crested Guineafowl in other places in Africa. There is a very distinctive subspecies from these forests that actually looks remarkably similar to a male Congo Peacock: both are large, plump, dark blue gamebirds with long necks, bare red throats and funny crests on their heads. It would be very easy to confuse these two among the leaves in the gloominess of the forest interior. Maybe it had just been a Crested Guineafowl I had seen in my peripheral vision. After all, what were the chances of seeing my target bird on my first day in the forest?

I was encouraged by this encounter and it felt easy to walk the four kilometres back to camp. I would try here again tomorrow morning, but this time I'd come earlier. However, the chance arose to accompany my wife with her bonobo research, and it was a few days before I made it back to that exact spot again. I was not yet confident enough of the trails to navigate the hour's walk alone in the dark, so I arrived only after daybreak, and began some scouting around.

Playback, a technique used by researchers and birders to draw secretive birds into the open, involves playing the male territorial song of a species in the hope other members of that species will come and investigate the intruder in their territory. If overused, it can cause disturbance to the resident birds and often, after a while, they largely stop responding: a situation that can arise in well known birding localities. However, for field surveys and birding in remote areas, and if used in a targeted and balanced way, it is a very important technique for revealing otherwise hidden birds. I knew that having the song of my quarry would be essential. And, very fortunately, a friend of mine had managed to obtain a recording of the song of a Congo Peacock from Antwerp Zoo, a descendent of the birds trapped decades earlier. Despite the tinny quality and people talking in the background, the structure of the song could be heard clearly, and I was sure it would work.

I prepared my speakers and started a bout of playback not far from where I had seen the scratching in the leaf litter. I must admit that I expected a quick response. A booming reply and maybe even a male running along the trail towards me. Nothing happened though. I waited and tried again a few times over the next few hours. It was becoming hot and sticky and the sweat bees were already clustering in the corners of my eyes and mouth. Maybe the heat had something to do with the lack of replies. Next time I would come earlier. Some of the early literature had described the peacocks singing at night, and so just after dawn was my best realistic chance. I had to master the network of trails to make sure that I didn't get lost in the darkness, but in a few days, I was confident enough to leave just over an hour before first light and hope that I didn't run into any forest elephants in the pitch dark.

The changing of night to day in the African lowland forest is an assault on the ears. The cacophony of crickets and hooting Chestnut-backed Owlets slowly changes to the predawn wake up calls of the louder primates, with whoop-gobbles of Black Mangabeys and shrieks from distant Bonobos sending chills down the spine. More comical are the calls of Great Blue Turacos echoing through the treetops like the stuttering starter motor of an impossibly giant car, competing with the hooting and booming of barbets, while the more delicate and complex songs of the flycatchers, sunbirds and robins fill in the gaps. Some birds I only ever heard during this short 20-minute bout of singing before dawn, and despite squinting up towards the dark overhanging branches and the bright sky distantly above, I never saw or heard them any other time. Others had their own specific times, such as the male Thick-billed Cuckoo, only ever calling at about 10:00 each morning, doing a big looping display over the canopy in his attempts to attract a partner (she would ultimately sneak onto the spiderweb-covered nest of a Rufous-bellied Helmet-shrike to lay her own egg).

I arrived at the spot just before dawn and the timing felt better than the previous occasion. I played back the song on the large speaker attached to my belt. I didn't get a response, so I waited a bit more, and then turned up the volume and played it again. No reply. After another hour of waiting and the occasional playback, it was already starting to get warmer and it soon became clear my strategy wasn't working. I explored for a while nearby, watching a flock of foraging birds and some monkeys, and then, on my way to back to camp, I half-heartedly tried playing the song again when passing by the original spot.

It sang back. I was completely unprepared.

The sound came from about 80 metres deep into the forest. The poor quality recording that I had didn't prepare me for the power of the sound. In the same way that you feel an elephant's rumble or a lion's roar, the song of the Congo Peacock is so loud and so reverberating that it literally shakes your bones. It is a sound unlike any other I have heard. It is hard to describe what it sounds like, although *Birds of Africa* makes an attempt with 'rro-ho-ho-o-a'. My best attempt at a description would be the loudest peacock call you can imagine mixed up with choir organ pipes.

I fumbled my directional microphone and minidisc, completely tangling the cables in an attempt to record its next volley, but it had already gone quiet. I knew that if I rushed in towards it, I would surely scare it away. So, I tried to keep as still as possible and played back the song again, hoping it would sneak closer for a better view of its potential rival. I couldn't believe my luck, there was a Congo Peacock somewhere in the leaves in front of me, very close and no doubt coming closer. I was on edge. I couldn't believe that I was going to see it after only a week in the forest!

The excitement slowly turned to disappointment. After an hour and another few playbacks, I realised it must be gone. I would try again tomorrow. I explored another area and only got back into camp in the late afternoon, time enough to wash off in the stream and hear the daily flyover of Spot-breasted Ibis at dusk. Later, Vermiculated Fishing Owls would call from along a nearby river with otherworldly Nkulengu Rails acting as the supporting cast (one book describes their song as 'sounding like a dancing conga-line going through the forest', and I can't improve on that).

Later that night it started raining heavily. The roar of the water on the leaves made it impossible to sleep, and the leafy shelter did little to stop water soaking into our dome tent. After a few hours, the rain stopped, and everything was still, besides the occasional explosive snapping of distant tree branches, overburdened by the weight of thousands of water droplets. I managed a few hours' sleep before groggily putting on my boots and heading off into the darkness.

Small streams were gushing everywhere and the big river had overflowed its banks. The small trails started getting soggier and soggier and I soon found myself wading through water. I had earlier given up on trying to use an old GPS below the forest canopy and relied on a hand-held compass to keep my sense of direction. The small tracks, initially made by elephants and now also used by hunters, were very narrow and because I couldn't see the paths under the water I started to get confused about exactly where I was going. A few times I ended up sloshing off the paths deeper into the forest but soon realised and luckily was able to backtrack each time. Eventually the water started to get shallower and soon I was back on dry ground and able to make fast progress again. I had almost reached my spot when I realised the path was blocked: a giant tree had fallen across the trail. In the darkness I couldn't see how far it extended in each direction, and the trunk was too thick for me to climb over. Initially I tried the left but got completely stuck in the side branches, so I eventually attempted to make my way around the right, and seemed to make some progress, slashing some branches and climbing under others. I soon realised, out of breath and completely soaked, that I must have moved past the tree, although I had no idea exactly where I was or how to find the tiny continuation of the trail on the other side in my torchlight. Above me the whoop-gobbles announced the coming dawn. I stumbled a few metres forward in panic, and then realised I was actually on the trail, and raced onwards. I was relieved to round the sharp bend in the trail and arrive at my spot.

The prospect of finally seeing the peacock was exciting. However, there was no repeat of the previous day's acoustic performance, and no signs of movement. Slowly anticipation turned to disappointment. I sloshed back to camp.

The following day I spent with my wife but the morning after that I was back at the spot, even earlier than before. I had been a bit disappointed that my previous attempt had been so quiet, but maybe it had been the rain, so I was again full of anticipation on the walk in. After two hours on tenterhooks with no signs, I began to question my strategy.

The peacock almost caught me off guard when it sang again.

But this time, I was even more encouraged. Firstly, it called from exactly the same place as earlier, strongly suggesting to me that I had found its core territorial calling area, giving confidence to my strategy, and secondly, this time I was prepared, and with my trusty directional microphone I recorded its song. And as anyone who records bird songs will know, there are very few birds that will not come to investigate a playback recording of their own personal song.

The game was on again. I waited a moment, and then played back the song that I had just recorded. I expected the bird to come quite quickly. But it didn't call back, and although I almost thought I could hear some rustling in the undergrowth, I couldn't see much through the layers and layers of leaves. Should I try and sneak up to it, and maybe catch it in its calling area? Or be patient and keep luring it? I tried putting a foot forward deeper into the forest, but a small stick cracked, and I decided to stay where I was. Half an hour must have passed. Had I chased it away? Why didn't I just rush towards the sound and try and glimpse it before it disappeared?

What happened next is still one of the most exhilarating moments of my entire life. The peacock sang again. Not in the same place, but this time just a few metres in front of me, just behind a few leaves. It felt as if the ground shook and my entire thorax reverberated with the power of the call. Although I tried to remain absolutely frozen, I was soon shivering uncontrollably.

I imagined I could see its shape – there it was! In a few moments I would see it sneaking through the leaves and maybe even across the forest trail ahead of me. Time seemed to stand still. I could hear the leaves crunching under its feet. But I couldn't make out any detail and the harder I tried to focus my eyes, the more I just saw shadows. I waited as long as I felt

I could and then parted the saplings. But it was already gone.

I spent hours looking all around. It had completely vanished. How could a giant brightly coloured peacock hide behind a few flimsy saplings and how could I not have seen it? I felt sick in my stomach initially. But that turned to hope. If it had come that close once, it would do it again, and I had many more opportunities to see it, I was sure.

I have never heard a Congo Peacock again since that morning. Nor have I glimpsed any further shadows in the undergrowth that I thought might possibly be it. I didn't yet know that though.

I became more and more obsessive in my attempts to try and see it. Later I cut a trail 80 metres deeper into the forest where I imagined its calling place was, carefully smoothing out little sticks and lianas so I could sneak rapidly along it without making a noise. I spent several early mornings there, playing back the song, and also just sitting for hours, as still as could be. Once, a Dwarf Kingfisher landed a metre from me; another time a Yellow-backed Duiker wandered past about three metres away and didn't even see me. My tolerance for the hypodermic bites of the forest-dwelling tsetse flies would depend on my mood, and on some days they would get the better of me and I'd eventually make a hasty retreat back to camp.

One morning I was sitting there scanning when suddenly my heart started to beat faster and for a moment I felt paralysed. I had thought I was alone in the forest and far from any people, but somebody was standing just behind me. I heard them take a step closer so I swung around to confront them. The Bonobo jumped back herself but kept watching me with a mixture of concern and confusion, as then, seemingly recognising me, she quickly relaxed and ambled past me as if I wasn't there. I recognised her too: she was one of the matriarchs of a group that my wife was studying and I'd already come face to face with her on one of my first days in the forest. More shapes appeared out of the leaves and soon her whole troop was slowly moving past, interacting with each other as if I wasn't there. For a while I completely forgot about my search.

I was getting increasingly desperate. I tried running along the trails in the hope of catching one dashing off the trail. Grant's Bluebills and Fire-crested Alethes dived into the leaves, pathfinder butterflies shot along ahead of me, giant green damselflies flashed off to the side, flocks of Crested Guineafowls scattered in pandemonium, and Blue-headed Wood-doves sat frozen for a millisecond before bursting off. No peacock.

The old literature, from examining the stomach contents of trapped specimens, reported that fallen fruit is an important component of the peacock's diet and this gave me a new idea. The big troops of monkeys that moved through the trees were messy eaters and half-eaten fruit would rain down as they passed overhead. I already knew that the small forest antelope depend on this bounty from above and would follow the daily movements of the primates. Maybe the Congo Peacocks would do the same? Although I thought I was quite stealthy, the monkeys would almost immediately spot me sneaking below them, and seemed to be mocking me with their alarm whistles and clicks before quickly disappearing through the treetops. With a bit of patience, I was soon able to follow them, mostly undetected. Once, as I sat against a log, a Blue Duiker, a dwarf antelope, walked by so closely, snuffling for fallen fruit in the leaf litter, that I could have reached out and touched it. No peacock.

My time in the Congo was coming to an end. It was Christmas Day, and the last morning I had on my own in the forest before I had to head back home. I had been planning this day for a while. One concern I had was that the peacock was getting used to the sound of my recording, a common problem with tape-luring, and so I had avoided any playback around the core site for about week now. My plan was to surprise the bird with one last bout of playback, hopefully piquing its curiosity and getting it to drop its guard. I had come so close before and felt sure it would work this time. I had never been as physically or mentally prepared as this morning. I even promised my wife I'd be back for Christmas lunch.

I walked there in the dark. I snuck along my specially prepared path to the call site. I waited silently. And then I played the song. The call from my speaker echoed through the forest. I was on heightened alert. I was convinced that a peacock was going to appear at any moment.

After an entire morning on edge, I felt things slipping away from me when I realised that no peacocks were going to come. The over-confidence of a 20-something-year-old birder came crashing down. I collapsed on a log. I was overwhelmed by emotion, the lost chance and my inability to succeed in the biggest birding challenge of my life. So many disappointments in life could be blamed on other people but this time it was just me. Earlier in the month I had been metres and milliseconds away from what seemed like one of the greatest goals of my life, but I had failed to grasp it. I was shattered. I felt like my entire birding career had just prepared me for this one quest, and I had completely squandered my once-in-a-lifetime opportunity. I had pushed myself to the limit, walking over 170 km in total and being bitten by countless tsetse flies, and yet had nothing to show for it. I was beginning to lose perspective in the forest. I could not even get up off the log.

I looked at my watch: I had stayed longer than I said I would.

My wife had patiently indulged my increasing obsession with finding this peacock. I had promised her I would be back for Christmas lunch. My personal obsession was beginning to take its toll on my relationship, and I needed to snap out of my thoughts and draw a line under my efforts. I had failed to see Congo Peacock: that search was now over. But I must not fail to make it back for lunch with my wife.

I stood up, swung my backpack on, and began to run.

The depths of the forest understorey are gloomy and damp. Now and then, shafts of sunlight percolate through the canopies of the larger trees and illuminate the leafy forest floor. Butterflies gather in these sunny spots, basking and pumping their shimmering wings, the males vying for a fleeting dominance. As the sun moves across the sky, the angle of light changes and butterfly arenas disappear into darkness.

As I ran around the sharp bend in the trail, less than 100 metres from where I had been hiding for all these weeks, I froze in my tracks. Sunlight was pouring down onto an area of the trail immediately ahead of me, but I did not see any butterflies. The shimmering blues, oranges and greens were from something else entirely. One male and two female Congo Peacocks were lying flat on the trail, stretched out on the ground and taking up the entire sunny patch. They were basking. Their heads were lifted alertly, watching me, but their wings and tails were completely spread open on the leaves to allow the sunlight to reflect off all the otherwise hidden iridescent areas of their plumage. Initially they remained as frozen as me.

The royal blue glow of the male's neck and wings was striking, contrasting with his darker back, red throat and almost comical head tuft. The females too were more exquisite that I had expected, with rich orange-rufous necks and shimmering peacock-green backs. We were transfixed by each other's gazes.

Then the scene began to unfold as if in slow motion. The birds did not flush away, but keeping their eyes steadfastly on me, stood up excruciatingly slowly, adjusting and shuffling their feathers into place as they rose, and then, delicately, stepped out of the bright light and into the shadows.

And like that, they were gone. Slowly the butterflies started to return.

The weirdest bird in the world

By Susie Cunningham

Most birds, like most people, are visual creatures. They have large, bright eyes, prefer the light of day and react strongly to things they see, just like us. Although we may not realise it, I think this is one reason why birds are so popular. The visual world is something very fundamental we have in common with birds that we don't share with most other mammals.

Far away at the bottom of the globe lives a weird and enigmatic bird that breaks all these rules. It lives in the dark, has acute senses of smell, touch and hearing, and doesn't fly. Furthermore, it has eyes so tiny as to be largely useless. Even so, this strange bird is revered as a *taonga*: a treasure of the Maori people and an icon of its nation.

I worked with Brown Kiwi[1] in New Zealand for half a decade from 2005 to 2010. What follows are tales of my encounters with two generations of this, the weirdest bird in the world.

George the cliff-hanger

Kiwi lay famously huge eggs. They are similar in size to those of the wandering albatross, though kiwi themselves are only the size of a chicken. Brown kiwi mothers lay two monster eggs in a clutch at the end of a burrow, then leave dad to incubate while they recover from the ordeal.

Kiwi fathers hold vigil over the eggs day and night, for the 80 days they take to hatch. They leave the nest only during the darkest hours of night to forage. Part of my job was to nip in while dad was away, and candle the eggs to check the embryos were developing normally. Candling was nerve-wracking, involving balancing the precious egg on your fingertips and shining a torch through it from all angles. I'd examine the glowing networks of veins and shadows cast by the embryo in full knowledge that to drop the egg of this *taonga* species would be more than my life was worth! It was high pressure, but rewarding work.

Every year like clockwork the kiwi we called George would have a nest in the forest on the edge of a large swamp. His burrow was in an earth bank so steep and high I often contemplated whether it would be better to use a rope to reach it. His mate was a bird we named Kerri – an enigmatic creature who lurked deep in the swamp and who we hardly ever saw.

---

1 *Kiwi* is a Maori word. The singular is *te kiwi*, the plural is *nga kiwi*. Writing in English, I am using just 'kiwi' for both.

Kerri's egg production was totally reliable, but George's incubation routine was not. He was a dedicated dad who only left the nest for an hour per night, but you never knew when this hour would be. Some nights he would leave immediately after dusk, sometimes it would be three in the morning. Waiting for George was an uncomfortable business, entailing crouching long hours on the dark forest floor listening to the slow 'tick ... tick ... tick' of his radio-transmitter. The pulse rate would finally speed up when he stirred: 'tick tick tick tick tick ...' letting you know he was on the move.

I'd wait with baited breath for the sound to fade away as he effortlessly scaled the bank on claws like crampons, and then moved off into the night. I'd then make a dash for the nest, scrambling and slipping on the steep incline, to check on the eggs before he returned. Candling George's eggs was done with my toes dug into the earth, heels hanging out over space, heart in my mouth...

One night, long after midnight, I was waiting for George to get up. I'd been waiting since dusk, hours before. It was a still, clear, cold New Zealand night. I could see snatches of brilliant stars through the gaps in the forest canopy overhead. A batch of fledgling ruru begged like crickets from the fork of a Puriri tree and their parent glided low overhead on her silent owl's wings. I lay on the leaf litter with my radio antenna unfolded beside me and listened to George's monotonous transmitter

... tick ... tick ... tick ...

...

...

...

... CRUNCH CRUNCH CRUNCH!! At 4:45 am I was startled awake. George's transmitter rang out painfully loud through my headphones: TICK! TICK! TICK! TICK! Heart hammering, I cracked open one eye. I could just make out the shadow of a kiwi in the dark; pacing cautiously over the crackling leaf litter with long beak outstretched, snuffling the unfamiliar smells of polar fleece and mosquito repellent. George picked his way towards me and pushed his beak deep into my sleeve. He let out a violent, huffing SNORT! as if to let me know what he thought of me falling asleep on the job ... then turned and trundled away into the dark.

Mauro the survivor

In November 2004, George and Kerri hatched a tiny chick we called Mauro. He was two months old when I met him in early 2005, and already feistily independent. When I first saw him he was crouched alone under a fern on a ridge top, a bundle of furry black-brown feathers and pale horn-coloured beak barely bigger than a tennis ball.

Mauro was born at a bad time. In the summer of '04/05, northern New Zealand was gripped in drought. The soil in the forest baked hard and cracked. The swamps shrunk. And kiwi chicks starved.

My task was to monitor the growth rates of Mauro's cohort, catching up with them once a month to check on their progress. For months, Mauro did not grow. The other chicks his age steadily dropped condition, so that you could feel their little ribs through the staring feathers. Every trip to the forest there were fewer to find. Each little radio-transmitter collected from each tiny feathered corpse was a heartbreak. Our team pathologist returned the same report again and again 'death by starvation'. It was a desperate time.

But somehow Mauro survived. Rain finally fell in June and

he was there to benefit from it. Eight months old and hardly bigger than he was when I first met him, but alive! He was the sole survivor of all the chicks hatched that dreadful summer. He made his way into my heart during those horrible months and his picture still hangs on my office wall today.

Mauro is a unique bird in other ways, too. Adult kiwi can be sexed on size and beak length: the females are both bigger and longer-nosed than the males. With hatchlings, though, it is impossible to tell. We got around this by taking a feather from each chick and sending it away for genetic analysis.

The first feather we collected from Mauro came back female. I was a bit sad about this, because I'd always called him 'he' in my mind – he just *felt* like a boy to me. But the evidence was against it, so I dutifully began recording all his data in my notebooks under the name 'Maura'.

A year or two passed and Maura stayed small. And then the opportunity arose to have her sexed again from a handful of feathers she dropped during a routine transmitter change. This time, the lab told us she was a he! I was elated, I had my bird back. But who really knew? We had one DNA test either way, and Mauro/Maura was still a young bird. Only time would tell whether s/he would yet grow into the large size and long beak of an unmistakeably female adult.

At the time of writing, it is April 2017. Mauro is still alive. He has remained small, like a male. But he had an incredibly tough first year of life and it is not impossible his growth was permanently stunted. His beak is long for a male – certainly longer than the average for his population. But it isn't really long enough to be unmistakably a female beak. Mauro is now 12 years old, approaching middle-age for a kiwi, yet to the best of my knowledge he never seems to have found a mate and bred. Why?

Is Mauro indeed a real oddity, a hermaphroditic bird? Or is he (or she) just particularly secretive? Maybe she is laying eggs for a male we have never found? Or maybe he shares the favour of a female with another bird, and it is this second male who looks after the eggs of the trio? This would not be unheard of in our kiwi population.

The story of Mauro is like the story of kiwi generally. They're strange, secretive, little-known birds. They're familiar and iconic, especially in my home country of New Zealand. Yet they live their lives under the cover of darkness and they hold onto their mysteries still.

A tale of Nylsvley

By W. Richard J. Dean

This is not a birding story, although birds are a small part of it. While most of this narrative is factual, like a recently elected world leader, I don't let too many facts get in the way of a good story.

From 1979 to the end of 1982, I was the Officer-in-Charge of Nylsvley Nature Reserve, near Naboomspruit (now named Mookgophong) in Limpopo province. Nylsvley is known to many as a wonderland of water birds when the Nyl River floods out onto the adjacent floodplain within the reserve and the wider areas downstream. A diversity of water birds, some in their thousands, and some – the more exciting species like Rufous-bellied Herons – in much smaller numbers. Eurasian

Bitterns boom through the night in the rainy season and altogether the abundance of birds and the numbers of species is a rich hunting ground for twitchers that still have holes in their life list.

But it is not only water birds that make Nylsvley a paradise for the bird watcher. Three species of eagle nest in the woodland on the reserve, as well as several other smaller raptors, and a plethora of smaller species nesting in the woodland, including relative rarities like Barred Wren-warbler and Burnt-necked Eremomela. The large diversity of dryland species in the savanna woodlands on the reserve and in the surrounding area is impressive, and is such that in one of the early, if not the first, birding big days, Peter Frost, Warwick Tarboton and I recorded 225 species from dawn to dusk, and we travelled within a single quarter-degree square to do so. A record hard to beat. We went without lunch, if I recall, one of the hardships known only to the long-distance birder.

There were some unusual characters among the birds on the reserve. Like the White-bellied Sunbird that, every year, built its nest on a wire hanging from the ceiling in the dusty workshop on the reserve. It entered and exited through a hole in a broken window, and even when the door of the shed was open this was the preferred way in and out. And the Crombec, another 'wire' bird faithful to a single site, that built its nest in the lean-to where I parked my bakkie, and insisted on being parasitised by a Klaas's Cuckoo every year. And Nylsvley and adjacent farm lands is one of the few places where the yellow morph of the Crimson-breasted Shrike can be seen.

To cut a long story short, Nylsvley also had large numbers of 'game', Roan Antelope, Tsessebe, Burchell's Zebra, and lots of Impala, the latter an overpopulation problem that had to be dealt with every year by culling. The other large, high-value species also increased in numbers as the years went by, and had to be caught and sold to various buyers. At such times, one of my tasks as Officer-in-Charge was to contact the buyers of game caught on Nylsvley, and to prepare the way for receiving the game and to make sure that the strengthening mampoer or witblits was ready for the game capture team after their long and often traumatic journey. In many cases I was given a buyer's name and farm name – nothing else. I needed an array of phone books for the various provinces so I could contact the buyer by phone as the consignment of game left the reserve to give him or her an estimated time of arrival. Phoning on a party line is not easy at the best of times. Our Nylsvley party line had particular challenges, one of which was the neighbouring farmer's Italian wife (who spoke only Italian) who answered the phone every time when you rang the operator, or at any other time the phone rang. Trying to stop this was a mission in itself.

Anyway, moving along with the story, I went to see the local postmaster to ask for phone books for the various areas to which we sent captured game animals. He said the books were available, and I could get them, but the question of paying for them arose. My suggestion that the cost simply be added to our phone bill was turned down, and he suggested that I obtained a buying order (or money) to pay for the books.

Getting a buying order from the ponderous administrative machine that financed nature conservation at that time was not easy, and would be time consuming. Getting actual money was impossible. Anyway, cutting more from the long story, I applied for a buying order from head office, and after two months, a more or less average time for such a request, I received my buying order. I then went to the post office in Naboomspruit, presented my buying order and asked for my phone books. The postmaster looked at the provincial administration buying order with horror, and said 'we can't accept this – why don't we just put the cost of the books on your phone bill'.

Editor's comment: Conserving birds is awash with the most unpredictable and nuanced of challenges, even at the edge of an idyllic vlei!

A forest, a companion, and a bird or two

By Morné du Plessis

At the lodgings in the remote Bornean rainforests of Sabah, a peloton of staff lines up to welcome me on the jetty over the chocolate-brown waters of the Kinabatangan River. From across the waterway, I hear the melodic whistle of a superb Lyrebird. Trees drip with spectacular orchid blooms. A handful of dragonfly species cruise by flirtatiously, so close that my binoculars are unable to focus on them. I begin to realise that I may have arrived unprepared for the avalanche of splendour embodied in sound and colour into which I'm about to plunge.

Instead of tackling this expedition with a professional

birding outfit, I've chartered a simple boat guided by a local inhabitant who knows his way around. During the trip we'll travel for almost 150 km along the Kinabatangan River, through a kaleidoscope of hornbills, pittas and babblers, bearded bushpigs, orangutans, large troops of proboscis monkeys, playful pygmy forest elephants, scurrying monkeys, and small waterside villages. The meandering course of the river, which constantly doubles back on herself, means that we ultimately end up only 60 km from the ocean.

Although the spectacular novelty of every life form awaits me, I have one particular target in mind: the magnificent Rhinoceros Hornbill. This hornbill simply pinnacles a Bucerophile's – hornbill enthusiast's – most obsessive fantasy. It stands almost a metre tall, sports a massive curved bill underpinning a huge red-and-orange casque. These colours are carefully applied with the bill from preen oil obtained from the gland above its tail. The casque bends away from the bill to mirror its shape upwards into an extravagant horn that gives it its name. This is its primary natural habitat and I simply have to see one.

Every morning before first light Frederico, my boat guide with the strong Cambodian facial lines, and I depart so that we can reach crystal-clear tributaries in search of the sources of the various contributors to a spectacular dawn chorus. As the morning awakens there is every bird sound imaginable, from croaky calls to melodious whistles, flowing tunes to staccato snaps. I decide to try to deconstruct this spectacular south-east Asian diversity step by step, sense by sense, and ultimately sound by sound.

As we turn off the murky main river into the clear water of the tributary, Frederico switches from the noisy petrol engine to a battery-driven electric motor. Gliding almost silently, we clandestinely enter the worlds of others. Voyeurs, we drift into the space of the unsuspecting.

Tcharrr-tcharr-tcharr. The call comes from our left. I raise my hand, a signal with which Frederico will soon become familiar, as I ask that we keep our distance until we've satisfactorily cleared up the mystery. The call belongs to a Fireback, drawing a line in the sand for trespassers who might consider crossing into his territory. I watch it for a while, then make a feeble attempt at imitating the simple sound. I fail, and notice the scepticism brimming up in Frederico's Cambodian eyes. This makes me more determined and I put even more energy and care into the reproduction of my version of the territorial call. Suddenly four large pheasant-like birds pile out of the undergrowth and strut along the water's edge, their tails glowing like hot coals. I notice a glimmer of respect shaping in Frederico's eyes. He had not expected this to happen.

We move further up the tributary. Our next target, I gesture to Frederico, is a bird that groups two whistles closely together, then waits. Then two whistles, and a pause. High-low, and a pause. High-low, and a pause. Frederico looks at me blankly as I try to copy the notes and the pauses as precisely as I can. Although even I know that I'm getting the sound very close to perfect, nothing comes.

Five minutes later I catch Frederico widening his eyes and then rolling them back in exasperation. It's enough of an insult to make me determined to carry on. Ten minutes later and our protagonist stops calling.

Frederico has had enough. His index finger reaches for the button to start the motor, but my glare discourages him. In this business, such sudden silence is often good news, because it may well mean that the bird is responding by changing its position.

And this is indeed good news. A Hooded Pitta with powder-blue wings, deep red splashes on its chest and plumage of a variety of exotic hues of green alights on a nearby branch. I watch him produce those two lovely notes, and before he can complete the full pause, a female flits into view. She perches alongside the male while he continues the high-low-pause ritual.

I breathe pure helium from well inside seventh heaven. Not only have I been vindicated, but this is a mother of a special bird.

I can't bring myself to leave the Hooded Pittas, but when they eventually lose interest in us and move on, there's a brand-new whistle that needs investigation: it's hoarse, and ends with a melancholic trill. What can it be?

Frederico seems to feel that he now has to lift his own game, and he boldly suggests that it could be a trogon, one of six trogon species that hang out in these forests. I indicate that I want to see this bird, but Frederico shrugs his shoulders as if a sighting is best left to fate. However, I'm having none of that. After only two or three attempts at imitating this somewhat more difficult call, a Scarlet-rumped Trogon joins. The bird with its loud red rump, chestnut back and turquoise skin around the eyes and on its neck is just as nervous of receiving any attention as its African counterparts. It turns its back and looks mistrustfully at us over its shoulder, inadvertently making itself even more visible by putting its bright rump at centre stage.

A glance at Frederico reveals signs of deep respect growing in his previously unfathomable eyes. He is beginning to enjoy this. When I signal to him for us to move on, he points at the trogon and shrugs his shoulders.

Touché!

We wait another five minutes. It flies off into the shadows in its own time.

Frederico uses the petrol engine to propel us up the brown

main channel for tens of kilometres before changing to the electric motor and taking a not-so-clear tributary to the east. Soon the fragile forest cocoon gives way to orderly rows of oil palms. My rainforest bubble has burst and in its place are many square kilometres of spikey-leaved plantation.

In places there are, however, narrow strips of rainforest left along the river banks, and it's alongside one of these that we stop. Frederico leans self-consciously away from me so that I can't see his mouth as he projects a series of nasal double quacks in the direction of the strip. I try to imagine what strange waterbird might show itself.

As Frederico seems about to lose his nerve, two spectacularly large figures fly over us and perch on the opposite bank. Unmistakable in their splendour, a pair of Rhinoceros Hornbills have responded to young Frederico. His Cambodian features crease into triumph. He's pulled a mega-sighting out of nowhere. Our bond is sealed.

Bells in the reeds

By Vernon RL Head

Round tanks that gurgle in ponds, stirred by steel arms and paddles of sludge on a hill of sand, called to all the flies in a hazy lullaby of dawn, and a single pink line of feathers rippled tintinnabulations past the buzz, on its way to becoming a secret world of flamingos.

'Woolies makes a very good avo and chicken sandwich,' she said.

'I did make the coffee though,' I replied with a smile. This was a first date, at the beginning of all the new things that come with the honest lights of the hottest suns of love, and I had chosen the Strandfontein Sewage Works for our picnic of spotlights, not only because it was cheaper than a good restaurant, but largely due to the opportunity it presented for me to show off my joy of birds on a stage, highlighting my inordinate skills in finding them ... or so the arrogance of this kind of feather-dance is supposed to go!

⁂

Gravel tracks criss-cross, bend and massage The Works into a liberating lattice of meandering adventures. Never before, in the history of Cape Town and its Flatlands – linking blue-green mountains of delicate flowers and titillating vines on either side of hope and oppression – has so glorious a basket of reeds been weaved more architecturally by so vigorous and unstoppably furious a need to shit.

'Long may the food we eat create such a masterpiece,' said my girlfriend, swallowing an escaping slice of cucumber, rolling the plastic wrapper in her hands with a smooth slide of her palms, basking in a revelatory glow that twittered in the gourmet rustle of the place. (She has always been a committed recycler.)

The soft breeze coming off False Bay nudged us, holding our breakfast in fresh saltiness, pushing the heady scent of putrefaction faraway, containing it on that barren hill in the distance. I politely snapped a nutty-fruit bar (also from Woolworths!) in half, offering her a piece elegantly on a white serviette, and shooing a delinquent fly gallantly, as is done in the dance. I had chosen the quiet edge of a strategic pond – my favourite pond, so generous in the past with national rarities like Temminck's Stint, White-rumped Sandpiper and a regular bevy of rallids: the puffy jewels that waddle and then momentarily pop from deep inside the reeds on special days of stars – a strategic pond in the heart of Paradise, sprinkled in crinkled blues and crisp apricots of the sky. The chivalrous morning came slowly, scattering the light on the water in many ideas and futures. And it really was a paradisiacal place:

Lugubrious birds abounded in myriad quacks, whistles, grunts and chirring crackles that rattled a low cloud into wings; and from the whiteness above tumbled metallic swallows glinting reds and cobalts. In all directions – we sat in the centre of a great wheel, the spokes of which radiated out from our eyes to every vista – water glittered on feathers. I looked at her looking: 'Ducks do not bob, they fasten water to the earth like the buttons on a Chesterfield sofa. Grebes do not dive, they disappear like raindrops on a pavement of memory. Gulls do not drift, they glide like tomorrow if you care to see the other side of cities. Herons do not stand in wait, they contemplate like the buyers of avo sandwiches,' she said.

She sipped her coffee with a grin, blowing the song of mist off her lips, a tiny ripple releasing an aroma onto me tenderly, banishing my hubris forever. 'Do you know there are hippos here?' I said. 'The world is now a place of relics, some irrelevant in the way the appendix sleeps listlessly in the gut, some profound and fundamental, a beating muscle, bright in the gush of all that is wet and precious.'

This carefully managed system of ponds and pans in the midst of a vast – and charred – braai grid, welding roofs to roads, divided by the divided, had been created with much effort in response to an expanding need, a metropolitan destination for the synaptic sewer pipes of excess. Yet inside the process, somewhere along the route of flushing and filtration, inside the spewed fluids and rising bumps and dumps of garbage, a single reed had grown, resilient and strong. And then another…

As with all light that rises on a stage of wild dramas, a colour

– in this case green – became a brighter green, the brightest, opening bowing browns into glowing blues. As with light climbing up into high applause, a new crowd arrived. And so it was that I danced with vibrancy on my first date.

She said: 'Look at the tips of the reeds, look how red, jingling in little beaks and bodies.'

(In mitigation of sentence, the reader should know that, in the end, I would triumphantly propose marriage in a reasonably priced restaurant that only served fish caught in a sustainable manner. But it is clear and unequivocal to all who will listen that the decision was made *that* morning, when I heard bells above the tips of the reeds. [And it should also be noted, discreetly, that I often smile fondly now when going to the toilet!])

Butterfly bird

By Vernon RL Head

BUTTERFLY TREES CALL when the wind runs through high leaves, turning a forest into a swarm of singing wings for tomorrow. Nature's Valley is such a place when the light is right.

I walked there once with a tall man of silvering hair – his head neatly parted with considerations and curls that rested between old books – who once spoke to a drinking leopard at sunset; and who showed me how to look up inside the forest's mind, near the place of trogons that speak complicated words. He is a famous ornithologist: small creatures that look like glass had been named after his patience and his careful eyes, in the way streets are named after memories; in the way crystals sparkle when you turn them in the hand slowly toward wisdom away from cities.

He was crisp like a crystal actually, slightly curved too, and when he walked, the forest walked with him, bending to the tap-crack of his shoes rolling across dry leaves; all seemingly stretching at his touch, suspended for delightful and easy viewing, wavering for a sign of camaraderie that would always come from his smile. We follow such men if given fortunate moments.

His shadow was splendid and strong as a bough, yet spreading all the time in stems of new branches. What a pause he held for us in his hands of twigs and fingers of feathers. We had a group of birdwatchers with us that morning, he and I and the other trees, showing the names of things that helped make the song of that place for people. (Names can link curiously into a lyric, just like clouds link into rain and leaves link into drinkers of raintunes.) We laughed as an aeroplane flew past, a white line of ice far outside the forest, looking for someone else's world; faraway from our powerful green of that day it whizzed, ours a season of softness without speed and steel. This shade was not a world of hard things; instead it only wanted to fold, commanding glitter, recommending the spreading of eternal leaves.

The walk was about moving sound and air of purples and blues: deep air gave a new call to en-lighten-ment. That is the place of learning: the waiting-seat on a fallen trunk in the day-dark, slightly moist to the buttocks, moss-ed of spongy scents, mushroom-ed of textures that please. We waited for gentle calls there, within, completely within.

❊

A French gourmand – one of the greatest chefs ever known – spoke about the notes that texture gives a dish: crunchiness has a way of speaking to the tongue far removed from gooiness, yet both can come together on the palette as a team to enlighten; in such a way, light links with sound in a forest to release smell, unfolding answers, revealing the most delicate of birds that take you back to your beginning: your first grasp of melodies of hope away from concrete.

Numbers had tinkled down in gaps between branches proffering a delicate proof: standing in a row on a tight path of things that breathed, we breathed; a team counting answers. The earth has layers that go from hard to soft; black to the brightest white expanding outwards; deep stillness shifts into the glittering edges of a dance that yields the sun levigated, and there, then, the tiniest stars are crushed appropriately into the sparkling mists of a forest day: look up when you stand in a forest. Look up carefully, you are in a precious thing. Perhaps hold the hand of a birdwatcher; you should not want to be alone in that voluptuous connection to truth under tinkling wings.

Our leader walked on, then, creaking happiness: moss becoming moss again, mushrooms becoming mushrooms. The footprints too sprung up, reshaping the forest when I glanced back, reshaping sight and the past. 'Do not pick up that old stick; it is nobody's crutch. It is a place for creatures that do not limp. We don't take places with us anymore, that is for aeroplanes. We visit them instead from within,' he said to the group.

The forest floor crunched – and to be sure it oozed like goo too – under a headiness that held us in the water of trees. He pointed with his green eyes – birdwatchers never point with fingers, not even those that are pointed everywhere – he pointed at a leaf, and then higher, further up, he gave a thudding knock to bark; he leaned and bent in all the symphonic ways ever swayed by smiles, and we saw them all, one by one, preparing the forest for light with beaks of music. Birds of the Leaves. Big Leaves. Small Leaves. Leaves with bits of red crest, others with bits of gold. A lady abandoned her camera to a pocket, another surrendered her binoculars to her neck; it was enough to just look with closed eyes, waiting like lungs always wait for moving light.

Then, on the spin of tides and near the suck of moons, it happened. On the rise of continents and at the crash of vast voids a thought shone. Up at the top of earth-quaking shifts where new leaves waited for the sun, at the boundary of a bright green sky, and at the shimmer of star-quietness of canopy, held ever cloistered by hearts, ever cupped by the hands of our host, the zip and the flit of a distant thing sparkled. It came as a burst: a border was crossed beyond the forest, above our world to another, one dialect giving to the next in a puff of pollen. Drifting up and out to the future fluttered the wings of a Butterfly Bird.

'So high and so small in all that brightness,' a lady said. 'A forest is for all the world,' he said, 'however small the patch.' Just in the way this tiny bird reached – as with all ideas – into the turquoise, it offered generosity to other lands; the lightest, brightest turquoise ideas floated across all seas and skies then, over all rivers and divides, reaching all aeroplane-cities. The bird was a seed of translucent musicality made for wings, calling all to see the good sound beyond countries, beyond borders and routes in the sky. No more deaf sun without trees, screaming out of greed for burning space and the heat of more people. No more people please ... it called. No space left.

A little yellow-green bird with a brown frown hopped high and away from the biggest, highest tree to snap at a fly dusting bits of grey in a haze out there; and Geoff said to the group huddled in hands far below: 'Yellow-throated Woodland Warbler, watch it before it disappears with this last forest on the edge.'

Our world is in a glass vase

By Vernon RL Head

Across the deep concrete yard – painted green to look like grass – tumbled a small, white cloud, folding dust into curls of vernal dirt. Above, a tree twirled in the breeze, fluttering dishcloths, crucified underpants and colourful red socks that called to a single butterfly; empty pegs shimmered like brittle leaves on wires. A birdbath nearby, filled with old braai coals, leaked grey dust from forest cremations down to the distant past. A dustbin overflowed at that back door of flies, squeezing a head off a plastic bottle with a slow pop of gas. And still the white feather rolled on, tumbling toward the wall, tumbling … downy, soft and detached from yesterday.

A day of numbers began then, right away: the wondrous

dance with time, endless in discovery on the air of everything honest. Endlessness to all horizons came with that first gaze through glass, my eyes leaning out across the world in a beginning of something. I had commenced a search to see all the birds. Everything was out there on the other side of the window sill like wings that never stop, not even for the languid breath of patient dreams.

I had been watching birds since the call of the Rainbird shaking fire-eyes in the early mists of my grandfather's farm 30 years before; since the first teenage bushveld hunt with uncles for warm, dead francolins in the orange sands glowing from the chase (so many different kinds of hunting; so many different ways of connecting to the primordial past of birds); since those rugby tours at school, when no one, not even the coach, was looking for a boy's wanderings toward birds and their poems of truth. Yet on this morning – here in a spontaneous spring – my list would finally begin. I had joined the Cape Bird Club the previous day. I had just found out about the Big List, what a concept: all the birds in the world in a row that winds across valleys, seas, forests and over mountains toward the clouds: the numbers game; one at a time. One ... then two ... and ...

'Over ten thousand species,' they said in a chorus at the Club; and now there needed to be *my* number one. A deeply personal ordering. A time of feathers anew. Predacious longings on a journey to make a life.

❉

Windows are places of carved revelation for the birdwatcher, especially those on the second floor of interminably thick walls. My flat looked out across the tight road into a neighbour's yard beyond a high, white monolith made in Victorian times of misunderstanding, the only open space anywhere now, resting there on the other side of opportunity, below a flat mountain, on the other end of another divide; so much lost, so many layers fallen on top of layers, memories squeezed below a laminated city: crumbled animals petrified into asphalt. But not the birds: No! Ambassadors of the Pristine; they have survived the explosion of us, and, there, through the pane and the many shatterings, chance glittered in the sky above the circus: azure-lilac dawned of indomitable fluttered song. Freedom beyond walls held in their calls. And my new day came slowly, turning as one would the page of a precious book; turning like a lonely, yet glorious white feather on the air.

Windows are places of light for the birdwatcher; any window prisms the world, focusing forms into rainbows that speak aloft, refracting old times into clear sentences of knowledge that float. It is all about seeing, the locking of a gaze onto a bird, one at a time... Then comes a miraculous thing: the unlocking: answers on the unstoppable sky. I know all clouds never end, merely drifting on the slow pull of a patient earth, linking continents in birds. The List of Soft Shapes and Music is a way to that: a spectacular roaming. And it all started for me that day at a window. O what a glance.

Another feather slid on the spoor of the first. What a stage open space can be for momentary wilderness, even if just a crack in a city, proffering up to the clouds and climbing sun. And a third feather tumbled, lighter; more energetic still. So fierce is the force of equilibrium.

Windows frame life for the birdwatcher (our eyes are windows): the pages of the future connect directly to the ancient past through glass, framing an evolutionary vista. Just look. Really look. I tapped my fingers on that lens, slowly heating with the coming day, opening the frame wider, smelling the sun lift, the new glisten of angles and routes and coloured ripples that breathe. Calls came from all directions like a million tongues of joy.

Facets magnify distance. Just look through a window of diamonds. Any window, anytime, even in the rain, and there will be feathers shuttled on subtle shade.

❋

My first bird was a feather long ago, a nudge of a wing from thin, long, hard grass. Could I hold that as a living thing in my heart, I wondered. I never saw it again, yet I knew the name of its owner. I knew how it talked to the shimmer-reflections from clouds every day, and I watched it fly to the lugubrious lost soils of sunset. But then it was a poem-bird. Yet here, at the beginning of My Big List, beyond art, near science, another feather? I needed to see the whole bird now, much like a stanza is not a story or a fresco is not a great building filled by all the light, I needed completion of a form.

I would come to tick thousands of birds on the List eventually, thousands of connections with wilderness, thousands of followed narratives held in words that made a brilliant map across cultures and ways; I would be led for decades in this intimate trust across lands by dear friends that leapt to far dreams and celebrations. Now a feather, again? *Now!* Of all the moments! Why not a whole bird!

Perhaps it was an exclamation mark before the call? A wake up scream of heraldic pride holding strange new flags beyond sovereignties, a stamp for my new footprints beyond high walls, commencing the walk below great trees sparkling of the real green, on this new path, the one I had decided upon today?

Perhaps the sighting was supposed to be simple, incremental like thought. A symbol before the first bird? Maybe a feather is the essence of a bird in the way a leaf is a tree, and a flower is the scent of the world.

The first bird needed to be seen eventually, of course, as was part of the ritual, the capturing of an image – all the many calls in that coming light owned names known to me intimately, yet they did not count now – the first bird was for the eyes alone, to be a gift for the mind of all my futures.

And another feather came. This time heavy, dipped red, dragging a brushstroke across the concrete, green becoming brown in a stripe of delicate river-meanderings slowly moving toward the wall. Thump-drip, thump-drip, eddy, puddle, smear. The red, a weighted shadow pulling at the white, summoning death, the way carrion might be dragged on the day sky hunted like a feeding pack of clouds. Feathers of the torn!

I was drawn to that yard of dead green – a flatter slab of wasted earth had never been more loudly silent – picking up the deep dawn sotto voce, desolate like all we have flushed from fecundity, coldly hill-less above a sea of sewers. I was drawn to it because of the dancing stream of feathers.

❉

Then the first bird came down from the stars. Perhaps the last star of all the nights, silver-lead wings sharp into the day, edging clean and acrobatic like a perfect fish, a shimmer onto the floor wetly lit by shadows under the clothesline, it widened and widened, then, in a blink, snapped shut. Feathers lifted in a fuzzy wave, the concrete was swept empty of them, shiny now only in a wiggly line of red: a quiet, long dribble continued, the alighting bird walked forward making muddy marks. Then another seven bursts, more stars rimmed in metallic blues and purples; and necks puffed on top of walking curves, pink-footed, glistening in flecks of emerald, beaks catching gold, shining hard for food in sharp darts: Number One: Rock Dove.

Exquisitely common like the wide sky, they landed in a scattering of gifts. My list had begun, the clock ticked; time rose, lowering boundaries, winding and rolling and owning the way forward in an obligate rhythm. Birdwatching is all about time because time is life: the beating, thumping sequence: after one comes two, three ... then... And it is this journey we seek, reading each bird: species after species, like words making sentences, telling a profound story of diversity, unravelling the mysteries that shape. How liberating to ask why. How interconnected with breath is that question: like a trail of feathers in the dirt. Where do they come from?

Rock Dove: pigeon of Piccadilly and the whirling gongs of campaniles, turrets, spires and minarets; Big Ben Bird; shitter on pyramids, glass skyscrapers and the widest boulevards on Earth; fluttering cloud of every city blizzard, bluer than the bluest shroud on the luminous plastic palm trees of Dubai and Las Vegas; O Mighty Guano King (and Queen) of every bridge of every span: Cliff God of Our Urbanity. The Rock Dove rolls like the Coca-Cola can and roams like the SMS. It had to be *my* number one! Go figure! (As they say on American TV.)

Such a popular bird had landed on my list incandescently. Populist like Trump it pleases with familiarity. Bird of walls; of old walls and of the new and proposed. Bird of all our walls, even the religious ones. It flies and continues flying in every language and race. And perhaps bird beyond walls; bird that might abolish walls in the end. The Rock Dove landed – seven in all – in the green courtyard framed by the deepest dawn. Because it was number one for me I saw it freshly then, with new eyes: global eyes of linking. How important it was now. Number One was a sign!

The sun stretched and the house turned copper above the birds as they jerked about among the fuzz of feathers that continued to drift about them; the tip of a Victorian roof flickered. My window caught fire momentarily, twinkling lines of day across my room. And more birds came. More species this time. Number two was a House Sparrow from the Middle East, number three a Common Starling from Europe. Then a bright Chaffinch flowered on my Cape Town yard (descending from a foreign pine tree nearby), a bird of an old London garden singing to Cecil John Rhodes about Africa.

❈

I turned from the window with warmth at my back, and began to drum my fingers on the surface of a vase next to the bed, my other hand writing names of the birds on the new list, the table shaking thunderous thoughts. Cut stems of flowers tinkled like ice. 'Our world is full of so many similes,' I said aloud below the shadows of petals on the wall, shaped in colours and names: poppies from Holland, English roses, carnations from a Mediterranean island, a lotus from India and, finally, a protea with its peaky crown, all tightly caged, yet somehow all differently free together.

Rock Dove is now on another list, I remembered: Science's IUCN Red List, a conservation list that will never end, just like us. Two hundred and sixty million individuals, yet a shrinking species in its wild state. Our world is a circus becoming a zoo.

I turned, and a big bird, hidden all this time, lifted from

the darkest corner in the yard; from it rained white feathers. Vast wings flew fast, high and faraway, making clouds.

Speaking waves

By Vernon RL Head

Long beaches always seem to end in rocks clustered like bits of food in the corner of a smile.

Three men and a woman paused in the middle of a white curve, the late afternoon sun shaping a strange black sea-creature of probing points and spikes: legs and floppy hats morphed into tripods twinkling great lenses, heads blinking of long eyes that grunted, swaying in pendulous breaths; feet sprayed sand, balancing feelers of dreams of birds in the distance. It was hot.

The tide was coming in, looking for itself. Water sung in lungs, scattering expanding bubbles that became webs on a wide tongue near determination. The sea-creature shuffled slowly forward, alert to the moving bay of deep azure-green shining at its left flank, and upon which its shadow swum. Behind, a spoorline of thoughts left a trail that had sullied a once pristine memory of morning wind. (Wild beaches are empty canvases.) On the right flank ripples of kelp lay in a necklace of Braille for small purple molluscs. And beyond that the sand rose in gentle white hills pocked in bristles.

Up ahead, edged by the heavy scent of an ocean stirred by herbs of concern, and still some way off, whirled streams of white salt in the sky above flat rocks. Every 15 minutes a thick wave slid above a thin one in a long sigh, and rocks glistened, igniting the dance of stars. Quiet would then settle in the air until the next big wave spoke.

The perambulating creature moved slowly toward its feast. 'Food for the soul' Insincerity might say flippantly, in the way cheap cocktail-eyes admire chocolate-box sunsets under the bent silhouette of palm trees; in the way Ignorance thinks the 'cry' of the fish-eagle is the 'call' of Africa. But for this singular mind of many legs it was about the titillation of nuance in diversity: deep inside all the white was hidden a jewel of rich browns: the Sooty Tern. (A new bird for the Western Cape List in this instance!) A name among names: title among titles: the story told by the Sea.

'Ewa 'Ewa is what the Hawaiian seafarers name it. (I never did see it off Hawaii, but I did off many other islands of currents and relegations. Perhaps continents are islands too?) It is a bird sounding dissonance in a collective call, sparkling like waves over coral reefs of foreboding: a cacophony of powerful warning of bleached warming worlds afloat and lost. So much is gone

now. (When blue fades there is only black.) And it must be said that this bird has earned the right to shout, cracking oceans: it lives above the water in a home of reflections, soaring-floating for ten years at a time above glass, they say! Wings have never screamed like that before.

⁂

The black lattice of crinkled shadows plodded on. The sharp bits got smoother. Sand spluttered. Simon said: 'It's your tern turn Mel.' The creature laughed.

Once on the rocks tripods flowered: What a bloom! The birdwatchers positioned themselves firmly, expectantly in excitement, to begin. It would take time to scan through all the birds; much shimmered; a shoal indeed. The same was always so different. As if one wing had given a thousand wings, and one crest had given a thousand crests, flowing into things of countless tails that never ceased here; the vast pose of identicalness plumed into a sea: all the whiteness, yet so many different whites. Perhaps there was hope?

'Tern this way,' said Mel to the Earth of moving wishes.

A rock pool that held a foot pushed a crab up onto land. An octopus that held a crab became a rock. A small jellyfish – ship of long hooks – sailed between legs. Green algae accommodated a green cooler-box and a green flask accommodated a cup of coffee. A blue seagull – species irrelevant to the story – which had been bright white up until that moment, disappeared as shade, such is concentration and good coffee. A blue horizon became the sea and clouds funnelled light about like spotlights.

⁂

'A rock pool is an ocean,' said Anne with a teasing grin, clearing her throat, 'and as far as I am concerned you should take your bloody foot out of it.'

'I can't,' I said, 'my foot is caught in fishing gut.'

And, just then, a thick wave came in a soliloquy like one of Shakespeare's very long ones.

Supine in the city

By Vernon RL Head

Every morning a wide man walked along the edge of cars, the pavement holding that row of little windows in a picture gallery of dreams. His name was Big Show, and they said the asphalt glistened for him, raining in crushed diamonds.

(He would smell the steam coming from the hot tar in summer, muttering a soft song hovering of melancholy: 'This is the scent on its way down to the Bay ... this is the scent...')

He washed cars for a living in Kloof Street – a tight place of trendy shops, loud plastic wall signs, and shimmering restaurants below offices of concrete that made even more money. He washed things very well in all the smiles squashed between the fatty smells that overflowed.

On dry days he would be sure to ring out and rinse his red cloth above the bucket, pulling it across the circular edge like a tent of shade, so as to save water after wiping many bonnets, hoods and glass curves that glinted unusually. His long strokes were delicate, caressing, in the way a farmer might pull the bumpy earth with a rake before it spoke about the green, or the way a painter might reach across a canvas of extravaganzas. (He did rims too.) On rather wet days there would be no work, and he would spend his time thinking under the partial cover of a pink bougainvillea hedge that tinkled near a road sign that creaked, having been gently bent by a wayward taxi-bus last year and never straightened in the hurry and the noise. Cloudy days with a soft South-Easter (a breeze holding a mountain in the sea of little white dancers) seemed best for his soapy expressions. And it was on such a day that we met.

His hair, of the tightest curls rolled into long antennae, tinged golden under years of sunshine, bounced when he spoke. The big face of the big man owned nothing but knowledge and seemed connected to everything that moved; a smile of perfect teeth as wide as the street was set in the copper skin of his Kalahari soul; his cheeks shone softly, sprinkled in tiny bushels from the past that had long since ceased to grow. His yellow T-shirt – brighter than any daisy – was three sizes too small and read 'VOTE COPE'. And his round belly displayed a colourful belt made of last year's Christmas tinsel threaded through the loops of his old army-issue shorts. Most of all, his eyes glittered like the moons of all the dawns.

'I like your red socks, Boss; just like this lappie and the red hills near Ageneys where my father was killed by a bull when I was ten,' he said. (Most people introduce themselves with meaningless echoes; others give you their life in an instant like wilderness: such people change the world.) I asked him to clean my car; he had already begun wiping the headlights of fried insects, and I figured, 'why not'. The heat of that noon had given the water in his bucket a coolness that seemed most welcome as it sloshed onto my open sandals, soothing my toes. I was stunned by his clear words. 'Out of the blue' – as they say – they had come: an intimate gift of his past to a stranger on the street. A moment – each moment – seemed deeply precious to this vast man filled with freedom and no time to waste in a day. Too much to do and see everywhere, I would soon realise!

'I'll be back in twenty minutes,' I said, 'and I'll pay you then.'

An hour rushed past, dragging this way and that in the pull and push of telephone calls, bouncing emails, and so many SMSs wrestling for space with WhatsApp screaming to someone's Facebook friend, before I could leave the room on the other side of Snapchat and my wife's Twitter account ping that she didn't know she had; and I approached my car in the din of all the speed hooting tailbacks in busy recesses filling in the shopping trolley of my mind. 'Sorry I am late,' I said.

'No worries, Boss. Look, I have a present for you,' he said. The car was shining as if newly unwrapped from a shipping container from China. He took me by the hand to the rear, pointing a thick finger at the back window glistening under the afternoon light. 'Look at my art,' he said with a grin:

Sky creatures came, turning on a drifting world, unencumbered since the beginning of the first breath ever sucked from the sky. Magnificent plumes laced in greys and whites slowly slid from left to right on the glass, spinning in whirls that nudged giant feathers and downy puffs across verdant blue. I bent further forward, dipping down, deeply down, to see up. I looked lower to see higher than I had ever reached. And then they came, and I was alone floating on an ocean of solitude, my body cupped in the primordial past: black letters making words, spiralling in lost full stops, sharp commas and exclamation marks, linking into exquisite phrases on the air rained down upon my face of twirls.

'Swifts,' he said, 'look them dive for you. So fast nah!'

I reached for my wallet.

'No money thanks Boss, I been seeing your new shop and I been using the clock on the wall when I walk past the door,' he said, 'Time isn't mos free anymore except in the clouds.'

I looked up Kloof Street, to my left: High began the heart of Table Mountain, up there in the purple shadow of tumbling tears flexing cliffs of the wildest green I had ever seen: proteas, ericas and dancing butterflies came down the slope in a powerful and ancient scent of herbs. I looked out to my left along the funnelled line of cars; I did not see the glass or the concrete fumes. Instead: Table Bay glimmered in bursting dolphins and snoek, before the sands shook waking seals tickled by the kelp. My ankles shivered; my wet toes tingled in the cold water of the stream on its way to a vlei near an unsullied beach, and the pavement hopped in frogs and feeding francolins.

An African relative

By Alan Kemp

When you have been addicted to nature all your life and made your living by studying birds, it is hard to decide the criteria by which a personal bird-watching highlight stands out most from all the others. Does one choose repeatedly watching one's favourite bird, which for me in Southern Africa would be the Tawny-flanked Prinia for its confiding and energetic nature? Or is it the most enthralling bird you have ever tried to study, which for me was the spectacular but vigilant Helmeted Hornbill of Asia, where even finding a nest was a personal triumph? On the job, spending hundreds of days and thousands of hours following Southern Ground-hornbills was always an enthralling and rewarding challenge, but in the end all observations, however arduous, seemed equally intriguing. Raptors also attracted me greatly, but they yielded data too slowly to be of sufficient academic productivity. Yet in the end, my most enduring personal satisfaction came from an opportunity that combined hornbills and raptors!

To explain how and why this made such an impression requires some digression. First, at high school I learnt falconry. Then, as an undergraduate in 1965, I assisted one summer vacation in a study on Sociable Weavers in the Kalahari, which included the first concerted study on the biology of the diminutive sexually dimorphic African Pygmy Falcon that only roosts and nests as a lodger in one of the surplus nest cavities of the weaver. Later, when I started work as an ornithologist, I learnt that it has a close relative, also in the genus *Polihierax*, the similarly dimorphic White-rumped Pygmy Falcon, but this species lives on mainland Asia. However, hornbills also only occur in Africa and Asia. So when my hornbill work took me to Asia on completion of my doctorate, I met and later made a few incidental studies on the tiny but bold falconets of the rainforest canopy, smaller than the pygmies and separated from them and in the genus *Microhierax*. Then, 30 years later in 1996, the universe offered me a chance to look for White-rumped Pygmy Falcons. My colleagues in Thailand organised an international hornbill conference, to which they invited me, and so I wrote to ask them if they knew where I might find my quarry. The only information they could give me was that once they had photographed a pygmy poking its head out of a woodpecker hole, although at that time the only eggs attributed to the species were brown and taken from an open stick nest!

Fortuitously, the field excursion for the hornbill conference was planned at the Huay Kha Khaeng Wildlife Sanctuary and World Heritage Site on the Thailand-Myanmar border, which was exactly where the pygmy's head had been snapped seven years earlier, my Bangkok friend Adisak Vidhidharm was going to spend a week there making preparations for the group excursion, and he allowed me to join him. The excursion venue was in dry deciduous dipterocarp forest habitat that, at the end of March, the peak hot season before the start of the summer monsoon, most resembled tall dense *miombo* or mopane woodland, with plenty of bare trunks and saplings, and a dense scrub layer below. On our late-afternoon arrival from Bangkok we visited the regional warden Preecha Suntaramat and his wife Thannyalax and were excited to find they knew of the pygmy falcon. Not only that, but Thannyalax, artistic like so many Thais, produced her illustrated diary with paintings of pygmies dustbathing, while Preecha dived into his video cassette collection and produced sequences he had taped of both sexes perched and feeding.

Dawn found me out on the forest trail where they had recently seen the birds copulating and by midday I had sighted my target, and even found the pair's nest in a disused woodpecker hole. What excitement after such a long wait, and what luck to have several days left to learn more about the species! By dusk we had built a ground hide to watch the gnarled 24-metre tall *teng* tree (*Shorea obtusa*), the nest 10 metres up the trunk in one of a column of holes and then, besides the pair of pygmies, to see three pigeon-sized Greater Flameback woodpeckers return to roost in their other cavities.

The 14-hour days that followed, each topping 40°C by the afternoon, enabled me to establish that the female was incubating, the male provided most of her food and they each had a variety of calls and behaviours, including the tail-pumping typical of small falcons. Welcome interruptions came when cool water and a plateful of delicious Thai breakfast and lunch was snuck into the hide! The male always alerted me with a flight call as he approached the nest with prey, while the incubating female used a solicitation call as he came and climbed to the nest entrance to meet him or, if she felt neglected, popped out to hunt her own small prey within 50 metres of the nest. The most significant prey were the 'flying' *Draco* agamid lizards, snatched from stems and trunks but augmented by many smaller, presumably arthropod items taken from foliage or the ground.

I tried to watch the male hunt but almost always lost his small form among the dense trees and foliage. I did establish that he searched an area of at least 600 metres around the nest, and anyway these pursuits allowed me to enjoy some of the other birds within his territory, such as Green Peacock, Hill Mynah, nesting Hair-crested Drongo and three pairs of Shikra, Collared Falconets, migrant Black Baza and 10 other species of woodpeckers, five of them large. During his excursions, the male sometimes 'sang' a piping song to proclaim his presence, the only call that solicited a reply when I played back a recording.

So, on the morning of our last day, I used playback to try and locate any neighbouring pairs as an estimate of density. I had no success, but luckily at midday I was called to our camp where a male had been spotted and, soon after I arrived, he caught a lizard, ate some of it and then set off northwards carrying his prey. I failed to locate his nest, but did narrow it down to a patch of trees about 1.5 km from the study nest. Then, to cap it all, in the late afternoon, with guidance and equipment from two Israeli botanists studying flowering and fruiting of the trees, I was able to ascend to the nest. There I discovered a clutch of two pure white eggs, measured them and the cavities and, just before dusk fell and for the last time, watched the pygmies and their woodpecker hosts retire to roost.

In due course we published the results of our observations (Kemp, Alan C. & Vidhidharm, Adisak. 1998. Breeding of the White-rumped Pygmy Falcon. *Wilson Bulletin* volume 110, pages 71–76), and in a couple of other notes on small falcons intimated that the two species of pygmy falcon may not be as closely related as they appear. What final satisfaction then, 15 years after our study and well into retirement, when the first comprehensive genetic study of all species in the family Falconidae revealed them to be sufficiently different for the Asian pygmy to deserve its own monotypic generic name, *Nesohierax*! (Fuchs, J., Johnson, J. A. & Mindell, D. P. 2015. Rapid diversification of falcons (Aves: Falconidae) due to expansion of open habitats in the late Miocene. *Molecular Phylogenetics and Evolution* volume 86, pages 166–182).

Now, all that remains on my bucket list is to find and watch the only miniature falcon in South America, the Spot-winged Falconet, alone in its genus *Spiziapteryx,* that nests in Monk-parakeet nests! And remains the only falcon genus I have yet to meet.

Giving young hearts a reason to fly

By David Letsoalo

Growing up in a rural environment with lots of opportunity to explore really inspired my love of nature. As a young boy, I remember going down to the small dam at the bottom of the farm over weekends to fish and learn how to swim. We sometimes found a woven Weaver Bird's nest hanging over the water from a big tree. As naughty young boys do, my cousin and I would raid the nest for the tiny eggs, breaking them to discover the tiny chick inside. I also owned a pair of 'ketties' and although I was not very good at hitting targets, I would always go with my friends to try my luck shooting at birds. Other times, we would stick our little fingers into a nest only to find a furry creature inside – not the chick we expected but a rain spider using the ready-built home.

Of course, I didn't learn my lesson and soon tried to raid a nest again. I climbed up the tree and wiggled along to the tip of the branch, leaning over to work my hand into the nest when the branch broke and tumbled me into the dam. I nearly drowned and the experience finally taught me the lesson that I shouldn't bother birds at their homes.

I began to love nature, though, the more time I spent outdoors, and when I was working as a pottery assistant, my employer gave me the task of reporting the birds I saw coming into the garden. My inquisitive nature got the better of me and when she gave me a birding field guide for Christmas, I started to go out often to try to identify the birds myself. It was quite lonely on my own so I persuaded some school kids to join me on weekends and the interest grew to the point where they were even asking me if they could come along every weekend. They would report back to me what they saw during the week and I would try to help with identification even though I knew very little back then.

While I was learning about birds and their behaviour, I also got interested in plants and trees so I would join up with the botanical and dendrological groups in Haenertsburg and this is where I learnt so much, which I would then share with my young friends. We had a lot of fun learning bird-calls but when I started a family, these trips into the field became limited.

Over the years, I met my students from time to time and we would catch up with each other and what we have been doing in our lives. I recently met one of these guys and the first thing he said to me was that he was not hearing a lot of bird calls where we were standing. I started explaining about the difference in habitat between forest birding and where we had met, when I suddenly realised that the little information that I had shared with him when he was younger is still part of his heart so many years later.

This has been the case with all of the students I have worked with on the Birds in Trees Programme, the Cape Parrot Education Project and the local Eco-schools Grasslands Programme. Passion, enthusiasm and even a small amount of information can make all the difference in young minds and it is this kind of impact that I hope I can continue to make as I pass on the knowledge I have gained from the many experts I have met along the way who have been generous enough to share with me. Thanks to all who have inspired me and who gave my young heart a reason to fly.

The search for the elusive Buff-Spotted Flufftail

By David Letsoalo

THE WALK STARTED as we passed through the pine plantation and into the forest. My birding client was enthusiastic about spotting birds and ticking off lifers. As soon as we got into the forest, I started calling them out ... the high-pitched call of the Sombre Greenbul 'Willy come out and play' ... the scratchy sound on the forest floor of the Terrestrial Brownbul tossing leaf litter; continuously calling at the lower stratum of the trees was the Brown Scrub Robin and so it went on. I was straining my eyes to scan the thick canopy when I heard the shower coming down and immediately stepped back from the path of the Knysna Turaco who has the tendency to defecate every time there is any disturbing movement below it.

A couple of metres on, I heard a low call coming from the forest and he was thrilled to see the Narina Trogon. The walk is not just about birding though, stopping to touch and smell the trees, plants, ferns is just as interesting, as well as looking at mushrooms, insects and all the small things.

Looking overhead again, there was a commotion with birds of all sorts in a birding party. One wing flicker was the Yellow-streaked Greenbul; between the leaves, a Yellow-throated Woodland-Warbler was spotted and the bird creeping on the bark was the Olive Woodpecker male with the red cap. But the prize bird for the day was an elusive skulker, almost impossible to see. We got to the top of the forest and listened for the call. Other forest birds were singing from all directions and we tried to isolate the direction of that haunting low whoooo call close by. The one on the left was too steep to reach and the other was in among brambles and thorns so we had to head deeper into the forest.

As we got to our chosen site, the bird called loudly. Binoculars, cameras and lazer pointers were at the ready as we approached the little thicket. The bird was calling closer and sent us crawling this way and that on the wet leaf litter and us with no proper rain gear. I whispered, 'Get down on your knees and stick your head through here.' We crawled forward, getting soaked from the drops on the leaves and the constant drizzle. The call was now filling our ears. Whispering again, I said, 'Please crawl closer to me.' I could see he was losing hope but still wanted to see it. From the corner of my eye, I saw movement – goose bumps on my arms ... 'Look at the small bulb to the left of the thick stem below the leaf litter trapped on the twigs ... No, not that direction. Crawl here next to me and look at the prominent light to the right of the leaf litter. What can you see?'

'I see a small black ball,' he said.

'Keep looking at it.'

'I see it ... I see it,' he said, repeating it time and time again. I turned to look at him ... he was as white as a sheet and had tears rolling down his cheeks – tears of pain and joy. As we sat on the forest floor, stunned by the experience, I said to him this is why some of the locals call it the ghost bird – because it is never seen ... They only hear its haunting cry.

In search of the elusive Shoebill

By Rob Little

As a birder since at least my early primary school days, when I was invited to contribute a story for this book by Vernon Head and Carol Broomhall I was particularly excited because I had recently published my book on *Terrestrial Gamebirds & Snipes of Africa* with Jacana Media. However, it still took me a couple of days to contemplate which birding adventure was my most memorable experience. I could have told tales about how with exceptional guide and friend Maans Booysen we found the Lesser Seedcracker and Blue Quail on the Rio Savane flood plain in Mozambique; how Mark Paxton's little Jack Russell helped us find a family of Souza's Shrikes in the western Caprivi Strip, Namibia; a memorable trip up Mount Karthala, Grande Comore island to find the endemic Grand Comoro Scops Owl and Mount Karthala White-eye; how a number of expeditions still leave me 'pitta-less'; or I could compile many fun stories about researching the Grey-winged Francolin in the KwaZulu-Natal Drakensberg and on the Stormberg Plateau in the Eastern Cape. But after all, it is the fond memories of a trip to one of the home grounds of the enigmatic Shoebill that won the day.

Frans Schepers, then the Africa programme leader at WWF Netherlands, had proposed that they would support a conservation research project to secure the future of Shoebills and the Bangweulu Wetlands in Zambia. Shoebills are rare and localised throughout their range, preferring to inhabit dense undisturbed papyrus swamps, and they are threatened by hunting, illegal trade, nest disturbance, competition for fish and the modification and burning of their favoured wetland habitats.

Just as an introduction to the excitement of birding, I'm sure many birders will agree that when you are below the 500 lifer species milestone for southern Africa, we have all paged through Ian Sinclair and Peter Ryan's *Birds of Africa South of the Sahara* or one of our fabulous southern African field guides and glimpsed the holy grail species illustrations such as the Shoebill, Eurasian Bittern, Ring-necked Francolin, Streaky-breasted Flufftail, Barred Long-tailed Cuckoo, African Pitta, Lesser Seedcracker, etc. and just paged on regrettably thinking 'well I probably won't ever see one of those'. However, having slogged up the ladder garnering more lifers, can I suggest that you avoid falling prey to that defeatist trap. Rather hold your chin up and be positive; after all, those elusive birds are indeed accessible, one way or another. It is actually intriguing how one's bucket list becomes ever smaller and more focused as one conquers those elusive species that you once thought were as good as mystery birds. But dare I still mischievously suggest that pittas are extinct in southern Africa.

Although my story is about an adventure in search of the vulnerable Shoebill during our project initiation trip to Zambia in October 2010, I would like to also share a snippet on the delightful birding in Kasanka National Park on the way to the Bangweulu Swamps. After three flights from Cape Town, I was delighted to be met at the Kasanka reserve airfield by Frank Willems, who was then the head ecologist for the reserve. After a relaxed evening at the main camp glibly chatting about what lifers I might find in the morning, I awoke and walked out of my hut to see Frank tending to his morning duties. I immediately interfered, asking him if there were any special birds around the camp, to which he responded, 'which one do you want to see first – I just saw Fawn-breasted Waxbills at the office, a Böhm's Flycatcher is often around the weaver nests over the garages and I can hear an Anchieta's Barbet calling over there.' Well, what a question, and that's how birding was going to unfold at Kasanka – let's get them!

After breakfast we headed for the renowned Fibwe Forest where the famous Straw-coloured Fruit Bat colony resides. On the way, Pale-billed Hornbills and Ross's Turacos flopped around in the trees. Can you believe it, Ross's Turacos were just incidental sightings along the way?! Arriving at the edge of the forest, similar to how easily lifers were offered back at the camp, Frank casually announced that 'the Böhm's Bee-eaters are over there, I can hear a Brown-headed Apalis above us, and a Purple-throated Cuckooshrike has just landed in that tree.'

Overall, Kasanka was a frenzy of lifers and my head was

spinning, literally and figuratively, until it was time to catch the light plane for a short flight to the Bangweulu Swamps. While I guess there are many 'off the beaten track' places in Africa where one can indulge almost spontaneously in numerous lifers, it was just amazing to experience it at Kasanka. While there, with Frank's passion for Kasanka and my lifer foraging frenzy, we decided to do a story, 'Kasanka: More than just bats', which appeared in *Africa Birds & Birding* (2011 volume 16(5): 60–65).

Approaching the Bangweulu Swamps we first buzzed the rustic Shoebill Camp airstrip to alert a large herd of Black Lechwe that we wished to land. We checked in at Shoebill Camp, which was most fitting to give us the best possible chance of seeing those elusive prehistoric-looking creatures. The enthusiastic camp staff ensured us that one of the best ways to see a Shoebill was to go to a nest. The camp guide informed us unassumingly that we could go most of the way by Land Rover, then we would 'paddle' or punt our way with mokoro boats, which are wooden dug-out canoes, for about a quarter of the way and that the final stretch would be on foot through the swamp. Well that sounded relatively harmless and certainly doable to see one of Africa's top bucket-list species. The Land Rover ride was expectedly bumpy but as in Kasanka we again feasted out on lifers along the way. For me the most memorable were Sooty Chats, Swamp Flycatchers, Blue-breasted Bee-eaters and Katanga Masked Weavers. The mokoro section was mostly a case of trying not to fall overboard, but it also produced myriad fascinating reed bed frogs and the occasional small snake. The 'fun' began with the walk through the final papyrus reed bed section. The water was almost crotch level and the upper 15 centimetres or so consisted of a dense floating raft of loose plant material. This meant that to make headway one had to lift one's foot out of the water and over the floating vegetation before taking each step forward. Well, I nearly died of exhaustion! By the time we approached the nest site, I was weakly pulling myself through the papyrus and threatened to give up many times only to be encouraged onward by Frank and the others. I am still convinced that I lost a few years of my life in that swamp, but the final outcome was amazing. Breaking through the last patch of reeds we came upon the massive floating platform nest with a fledged chick that took to the air on gigantic wings.

The impressive size of two flight feathers that had been shed recently on the nest was almost unbelievable. Each one of these feathers weigh almost three times the entire body weight of the smallest bird in the world, the Bee Hummingbird. After savouring the experience of being at this nest site and taking a few photos for the record it was time to head back – well, I almost died again! All I can say is that I forever have huge admiration for the people that stomp around in those swamps, and I guess also for Ralf Mullers who we condemned to the swamps for two years to conduct our Shoebill conservation research that would later lead to a management plan for the conservation of Shoebills in the Bangweulu Wetlands to be implemented by the Zambia Wildlife Authority (ZAWA) and the African Parks Network.

The key issues regarding Shoebill conservation were to elevate the avi-tourism value of the Shoebill and to find a balance between fishing pressure and disturbance levels so that Shoebills can thrive and therefore add an economic incentive to their role in the wetlands. Ralf also published informative articles on 'grey ghosts of the wetlands' in *African Birdlife* (2014 volume 2(5): 24–30) and on 'Shoebills and people in the Bangweulu Wetlands, Zambia', in the NGO magazine *Environment* (2015 volume 21: 17–18).

On the flight back to Lusaka, just to end the excitement and intrigue, the trip in a little four-seater plane also had its moments. I was kept awake by comments to the pilot that 'you are going into the Congo, turn left'. To which the pilot would respond 'oh okay, this onboard GPS (or whatever those flight instruments are called) is a bit wonky'. This happened again and again, but in the end we stayed somewhat on track for Lusaka. I was in any case enjoying the spectacle of low-level flying over vast tracts of tropical forest. Then the Lusaka airport flight control tower started to bark muffled messages through the headsets about our approach to which the pilot responded 'copy'. When we asked him if he could actually hear what they were saying, his response was a casual 'no, but if you say "copy" they leave you alone for a while'.

And so finding the elusive Shoebill has remained one of my favourite lifers. To the point that a few years later my sons Bryan and Ian went on a trip to investigate Blue Swallows on their wintering grounds in Uganda and made the naïve mistake of letting me know that they had seen a Shoebill. It had taken me 55 years of my life to see the bird and they had now seen it at only 34 and 33 years old, respectively. On their return to South Africa I was phoned by the Pietermaritzburg hospital to say that Ian was in the intensive care unit with life-threatening malaria. Considering his recent 'casual and somewhat cheeky' admission of seeing a Shoebill, and to the amazement of the hospital staff, all I could say was 'let him suffer a bit – he deserves it'. Obviously, I called back a little later to check that all was well and that I didn't need to rush to Pietermaritzburg. Following this, my boys gave me a stunning commissioned 90 x 90 cm painting of a Shoebill by John Michael Metelerkamp for my 60th birthday, which by the way was celebrated at the Pongola River Company camp on the banks of the Pongola

River in Zululand, accompanied by Pel's Fishing Owls and African Finfoots. The painting has pride of place above my seat at our dining room table.

All in all, birding has given me an added purpose and has excited me through many holidays and field trips. While the Big 5 'mammals' are indeed special, and have certainly done their bit in attracting tourists to southern Africa, I have always wondered how people wind their way through conservation areas with the ultimate and almost sole aim of locating those large mammals. I have often taken pleasure in informing tourists when asked while parked along a park road 'what are you looking at?' by responding 'we are admiring that stunning Green-winged Pytilia', to which they usually look disgusted and drive on!

References / Further reading

Mullers, R. 2014. Grey ghosts of the wetlands. *African Birdlife* 2(5): 24–30.

Mullers, R.H.E., Amar, A. & Little, R.M. 2014. Shoebills and people in the Bangweulu Wetlands, Zambia. *Environment: People and conservation in Africa* 21: 15–16.

Willems, F. & Little, R.M. 2011. Kasanka: More than just bats. *Africa Birds & Birding* 16(5): 60–65.

A thing with feathers

By John Maytham

ONCE UPON A TIME I was travelling with friends in an open Land Cruiser in the Sabi Sands. We had to brake hard to avoid a large (perhaps 4.5 metre) African Rock Python that slithered into the road, moving with unusual speed, and with what seemed to be great determination. Something we understood better with hindsight. It settled on the other side about 15 metres into the long grass. To its left a breeding herd of Impala was slowly approaching the still and camouflaged snake. Among them were roughly a dozen recently born young ones, many still unsteady on their newly discovered, wobbly legs. One mother and calf were heading inexorably towards the python. We watched in awful fascination. We wanted it to happen; we didn't want it to happen. It did happen. The baby got close enough; the python reared its upper half and within seconds coiled about a third of its sinuous length around the baby Impala, and leisurely, but surely, squeezed it to death. The mother circled anxiously, bleating helplessly in chorus with her baby. Its bleating stopped, the mother's didn't. Then the python performed that almost magical trick of opening its upper and lower jaws wide with a gymnast's ability, and started, with painstaking slowness, to swallow its meal. (I have since learnt that herpetologists call this the pterygoid walk – the snake 'walks' its skull over the meal, slathering it constantly with saliva to ease the passage down the body.) We watched the last tiny hoof disappear from view and the jaws realign. All the while the snake's vertebral column was billowing in and out like an accordion, getting the meal to fit perfectly into its stomach so the unhurried process of digestion could begin. Eventually the python lay still again, the mother Impala gave up her vigil, and we drove off. Some months later I told this story, with photographic proof, to a very well-travelled wildlife journalist. And in the best tradition of fireside storytelling, he capped it with a similar, but better, one of his own. His story was set in Botswana and began much like mine, but it had a better ending. Just before the last tiny hoof disappeared, a leopard appeared and took hold of it and a tug-of-war ensued. The leopard won and went off into the thick bush to consume its opportunistically acquired prey. The python, we presume, lay and sulked for a while before moving off to try again. My story was well and truly trumped.

I love birding for many of the reasons that most birders will offer when asked. Though most will look at you with some perplexity first – as if the answer was as obvious as the wing ornaments on a Standard-winged Nightjar. It's about being in nature – different geographies, different habitats.

The more serious one gets, the more of the world one sees. And birdwatching can be done anywhere: your own backyard, the jungles of Indonesia, or slap-bang in the middle of a metropolis like Paris. Within half an hour of scoping the Mona Lisa, you can walk into the Bois de Boulogne and feast your eyes on the likes of Black Woodpeckers, Short-toed Treecreepers, Eurasian Nuthatches, Goldcrests and five varieties of tits. It's about the challenge of identification; it's about the importance of preserving habitat; it's about the thrill of the new and the comfort of the familiar. And, for those of us who unashamedly describe ourselves as listers, it's about the numbers, which means it is also, to a degree, about the competition. (In my experience, always the friendliest kind. Although for several years I delighted in believing that I had seen a bird, the Sangha Forest Robin, which the man with the longest African list of all, Ian Sinclair, had not seen. I wanted to strangle him – python-style – when he told me two years ago, with gravelly delight, that it had been reclassified as a subspecies of the much more common Orange-throated Forest Robin.)

But there is another noteworthy reason why I love to bird, and why I love to hang out with other birders. It's because of the stories. Stories are, and always have been, special in my life and in the life of mankind. No one knows when the first story was told, but what's the point of developing language if you don't want to liven up life around that new invention – fire – with something more than grunts and gestures and facial expressions. (The good storytellers still retain this ur-tradition.) There is much scientific disagreement about the origins of language. A 2003 book on the subject, *Language Evolution*, edited by Morten H. Christiansen and Simon Kirby, described language evolution as 'the hardest problem in science', and there are numerous competing theories as to what sparked the development of speech. My personal favourite, just because of the name, is Dean Falk's 'Putting the Baby Down' theory. This postulates that *Homo sapiens* women couldn't take their babies with them when foraging like their primate relatives, because evolution deprived them of the fur to which primate babies cling. They had to put them down and leave them alone for a while. Language thus developed out of the need for a system of communication that reassured the baby that mummy would be home soon. But it is generally believed that humans started talking about 100 000 years ago, and perhaps that all languages – a total of about 5000 – evolved from one common language developed in Africa. And all of those languages have a rich tradition of storytelling.

When you're birding, there are plenty of opportunities for storytelling. Those long periods in the car getting from one stake-out to the next; the fallow intervals waiting for something to appear out of the reeds or from the sky while in a wetland hide; and the very fertile occasions offered for narrative by mealtimes, especially after a long and lifer-rich day of whipping the binos up and down and around. Birders are far from the nerdy, train-spotting, number-plate-noting old (even when young in years) duffers they might have once been portrayed to be. I have been privileged to bird alongside some notable individuals who have told some wonderful stories, most of them probably true. Oh, all right, all of them. Stories grand and humble. I have some grand stories of my own. There was the trip into the Zambesi Valley for the Angola Pitta, as it was then called. Yes, we saw it, up and close and personal, doing the text book jump from a low branch with the preert sound as it took off, and the fanning of the tail after landing, displaying the incarnadine vent. When it tired of showing off, it flew away, straight past me, so close I swear I felt, on my left cheek, the breeze caused by its passing. That's not the end of the story. Because she was tired and wanted to rest, one of our party left early to walk the five km or so back to the car. We birded some more – Livingstone's Flycatcher another of the specials collared – and then followed in her footsteps. Early departure lady was not there. And she had the car key. And the coolbox with ice-cold Fanta we were all craving in the 45 degree plus humid heat was in the car. It was in my fitter days, so I volunteered to run back along the track to find her, which I did, and then ran back with the key, and then ran back to her with a Fanta. A total of about 10 km – tougher than any marathon I have run. We told the story over and over again that evening on the verandah of the Guruve Hotel, eating peri-peri flavoured sardines on Salticrax and drinking Zambesi beer out of the hotel's only glassware, brandy goblets. It felt like dragging a baby Impala by the hooves out of a python's jaws, but the reward was much tastier. That happened 20 years ago, and the memory is as alive today as it was then, kept fresh by the many re-tellings – I hope not too many of them to the same people.

Then there was the time in the Central African Republic when our journey back to Cameroon was halted for two days by a massive tree trunk obstructing the narrow jungle track. One of my favourite photographs is of the desperate me hacking away at a trunk as thick as Ollie le Roux's chest during his most voracious Spur cheeseburger-eating days and doing it with the saw blade of my Leatherman. That was never going to work. In the end, a logging truck came along with a chainsaw, and we were able to proceed. But in the two days we were stuck, I saw 18 lifers, among them a Violet-tailed Sunbird, a Velvet-mantled Drongo, a Chocolate-backed Kingfisher and a White-headed Woodhoopoe. I wouldn't have minded being stuck there for another few days, but we were running out of food and water.

The stories that matter to me most, though, are small stories of personal birding achievement. The majority of my grand stories happened when I was in the company of other more experienced friends or professional guides. I am not a very good birder – I don't have the characteristics that an article on the Birdwatch website described as necessary to be outstanding: 'The eyes of a hawk, the hearing of an owl, a photographic memory and a sixth sense for knowing where and when to watch and listen'. I have moderately decent numbers on my various lists, and I am confident that each tick is merited, but I've had an enormous amount of help. So it is the ticks on that list that are the result of my going alone to an area, studying bird calls and bird ID before the outing, and then positively identifying birds *by myself* that are the stories I tell quietly to myself. I will never forget the sense of accomplishment when, very early in my birding days, on my first trip to the Kruger, I recognised the call of the Rattling Cisticola on only my second day. Similar quiet satisfaction settled on me on the day when I realised that I knew at a casual glance whether I was looking at a Wood, Marsh or Common Sandpiper. Or when through my binos I saw a bird perched on a grass stalk in a marshy part of Dullstroom, and knew with absolute certainty that it was my first Pale-crowned Cisticola. There is a story to be told about going to Strandfontein and having the Temminck's Stint pointed out to you by one of the helpful crew that had already settled in with their long lenses trained for that extra special photographic opportunity offered by this 7th-ever local appearance of the species. Or about being taken to a pitta stakeout in Khao Sok National Park in Thailand and spotting five individuals from two different species of pitta, Banded and Blue-winged, in one sweep of the binoculars from left to right. Those are good stories, but in my personal story library, they are written in a duller font than the one of walking down to Bridal Veil Falls near Chimanimani in Zimbabwe's Eastern Highlands to look for the Mottled Swift. I saw a squadron of the birds with their very impressive aerobatic flight pattern. Even better was the encounter with a wagtail bobbing around the rocks at the base of the waterfall, and knowing, immediately and without any doubt, that I'd just had the totally unexpected pleasure of meeting my first Grey Wagtail. And I didn't need anybody to point it out and identify it for me.

Joan Didion once wrote: 'We tell ourselves stories in order to live.' In my life, stories about birdwatching – the ones I tell myself, the ones I tell others, the ones others share with me – help me to live more richly. And the best part of my birdwatching story is that many more chapters, grand and humble, remain to be written. Maybe one of them will trump my python story, because it does irk me that my best story involves a mammal and a reptile, with birds providing only a musical back-drop to which we paid no attention at the time. Perhaps, one day, I can start a story with 'Once upon a time, I went to Myanmar, and next to a tranquil, remote lake I discovered that the Pink-headed Duck was not extinct after all' and live happily ever after.

Adventures in the search for the Karamoja Apalis

By Adam Riley

The crowded matatu (local minibus taxi) rolled onto the dusty streets of Masindi. I had been wedged in the back row for the last four hours and although my butt was throbbing with pins-and-needles, my mind was racing on what my next move should be... I had a dreadful foreboding that my Uganda trip would be spent on public transport like this, bumping from town to town, trying to find my companions.

My friends Jon and Shez Rossouw and Marco Sacchi were contracted to compile a bird-finding guide to Uganda and had already been in the country for a couple of months. Inspired by my earlier visit, they had invited me to join them for a few weeks. Just as I was leaving, my terminally ill father had sadly passed away and I wasn't able to fly on the date I was scheduled to meet them. Being 1998 and pre internet and cellphone days, I was unable to contact them. A few weeks later I decided to head up anyway. All I knew was the name of the hotel they had used in Kampala and that they had a vehicle and driver provided by the Uganda Tourism Board.

Once I arrived, I bummed a lift late at night from Entebbe airport with some Irish ex-pats who dropped me off at the seediest hotel I had ever had the misfortune to frequent. Here I was informed that my buddies hadn't checked in for many weeks. Frustrated and exhausted I barely recall climbing into bed before leaping out in disgust as I hit a wet patch in the middle of the mattress that could only have been caused by something unsavoury... Needless to say, I spent the rest of the night on the floor in my sleeping bag!

The next morning I made my way to the Uganda Tourism Board offices and was told that the last contact with my friends was a week earlier when the group was in Murchison Falls National Park. This massive park, straddling the Nile, has several campsites and lodges and is nearly 100 km from the nearest town, Masindi. Off I went. Just as my matatu was pulling into the taxi rank, one of the luckiest coincidences in my life occurred.

It turned out my friends left Murchison Falls days earlier. They had been birding in Budongo Forest (where I would never have found them), and were about to head south. However, Marco was suffering from a bad headache so they detoured into Masindi to visit a pharmacy.

Lo and behold, my matatu parked right next to them! Peering forlornly out of the dusty square inch of window that I was privy to, I spotted Shez's bright red hair just as she climbed into an old Land Rover! They were about to pull out when they were distracted by a crazy mzungu (Swahili term for a white man), screaming and waving his arms in a frenzy, as he clambered over locals to scramble out of a taxi...

Reunited, the next few weeks were jam-packed with birding adventures. We explored the length and breadth of Uganda with numerous unexpected thrills, from finding a new bird for East Africa (Black-throated Coucal) while camping in the lowland rainforests of Semliki National Park on the border with DRC, to nervously scouring the roads ahead of us for an LRA (Lord's Resistance Army) ambush in the out-of-bounds Moroto region near the northern Kenya boundary. However, the grand finale of the trip was being flown to the little known and remote Kidepo Valley National Park in the Karamoja region of far northern Uganda. Adjoining Sudan (now South Sudan), this park had long been off the tourist map and closed to visitors due to the danger of getting there, lack of facilities and the presence of the SPLA (Sudan People's Liberation Army) in the park.

As the Ugandan Tourism Board wanted the bird-finding guide to be comprehensive, special permission had been arranged for us to explore the park. We camped near a Ugandan military base in the south of the park, where the buildings around the camp were pock-marked with bullet holes from a recent SPLA attack. The Ugandan military had killed a few SPLA child soldiers who were poaching game in the park and a revenge attack had ensued! We had been told to restrict ourselves to the southern section of the park away from the Sudan border in order to avoid the SPLA.

Even without the threat of guns, there was excitement galore. The birding highlight was finding the mythical Black-breasted Barbet, Africa's largest and arguably most impressive barbet, seen by very few birders as a result of its awkward range extending from far northern Uganda, through South Sudan to northern CAR and Chad. We had lions roaring between our tents, making the very ground vibrate, and every evening a leopard coughed nearby.

Marco, an expert snakehandler, picked up a small snake one evening and made the cardinal error of not identifying it in advance as a Burrowing Asp. These wormlike but highly venomous subterranean snakes prey on moles and in order to strike them in restricted burrows, they sport specially modified fangs that are able to strike sideways and backwards. This means that however carefully you grasp the snake behind its head it can still get you and that's exactly what happened to Marco who was struck on his index finger. He spent the rest of his stay in Kidepo writhing in agony in his tent until our charter plane returned us to Entebbe a few days later. He flew straight back to Switzerland and was lucky not to lose his finger, but unfortunately he missed out on even more crazy adventures...

Late one night on a nightdrive, miles from camp, we ran out of fuel... We had been wondering why the fuel gauge on the old Land Rover we had been loaned hadn't dropped below half for days. Now we knew, it was faulty! Our ranger told us we had three options. Sleep in the vehicle, which wasn't ideal since mosquitos were buzzing everywhere and it was pretty chilly, or walk, either all night back to our camp, or a few miles further on to an army outpost on a hill. We decided the final option was the best, but the walk was rather arduous with big cats and snakes around, and not a flashlight among us on this dark, dark night.

Finally, the murky outline of the koppie appeared before us, but now a new danger transpired. We were approaching an armed military base unannounced in the middle of the night! Fortunately this was when our ranger displayed his brilliance. In his loudest bellow he began to issue forth in radio communication speech to the base '*Outpost Delta, Outpost Delta come in for Echo 12*' and was thus able to warn the night watch that it was friends not foe approaching the camp.

On top of the rocky outcrop it was bitterly cold yet the soldiers generously donated one blanket under which the four of us snuggled on the bare ground. It certainly wasn't the most comfortable night but still beat my Kampala experience and in the morning we were rewarded with a covey of noisy Stone Partridge – a lifer all around!

On return to camp the next morning we still had a full day to explore but felt we had exhausted all the options in the south. This is when Jon, who always pushes the envelope to the limit, decided we should lobby for an armed convoy to take us to the far north of the park, right to the Sudanese border. This was the site where the mythical Karamoja Apalis had been discovered. At this time, the species was known only from these Ugandan type specimens and a few records of a different subspecies on the remote Wembere Steppes in northern Tanzania. We knew of no birder who had ever seen this small, white-winged warbler that was restricted to dense stands of Whistling-thorn Acacia. At first the response was an outright negative, but Jon, being a very persuasive bloke, finally convinced the park authorities and army commander that the scientific value of such an expedition would be immense. Eventually they conceded we could try the next day.

It took a while to mount our expedition but finally we set off in a massive flatbed truck with 30 soldiers in full combat gear, armed to the teeth. Progress was slow. Before each river crossing half of the battalion would disembark and fan out on foot checking for SPLA ambushes.

Finally in the heat of the day we reached the Sudanese border and the zone where the Karamoja Apalis had been discovered. Here we started birding, surrounded by all the troops. Suddenly through the heat haze we spotted a line of ragtag soldiers approaching from the bushes ahead. As they neared we saw they were all youngsters aged from about ten to mid-teenage, armed with an assortment of weapons ranging from spears to old rifles, hand-grenades, AK47s and even a few rocket launchers! We looked around to see how our protectors were preparing for battle, but miraculously they had vanished into thin air without our even noticing!

So here we were, armed with just binoculars and bird books, standing down a notorious rebel army! To say we were terrified was an understatement. The SPLA approached with caution and we had no choice but to put on a brave face and appear jovial and confident. We stuck out our hands in greeting and after receiving reluctant handshakes, we began pointing to the apalis and other birds in our field guides. The young lads were bemused and fascinated; they recognised some of the birds, and were thrilled to look through our binoculars.

Once the amicable mood was clear the Ugandan soldiers started emerging and more handshaking ensued. After protracted discussions we were finally released by the SPLA, but not before we asked some of the rebels to pose for a photo with us in which they proudly brandished their rocket-launchers! We loaded back onto the troop carrier, relieved we were alive yet disappointed we had missed the apalis.

Within minutes of setting off back to camp Jon suddenly started screaming 'Karamoja Apalis, Karamoja Apalis'. At first I thought he was joking until he leapt off the moving truck and we all followed suit and, sure enough, we confirmed that this mythical bird still survives in its remote place of discovery!

This sighting was the icing on the cake of a remarkable trip, but ultimately it's the whole of the journey I'll remember. The unexpected twists, turns and excitement of the chase always make me yearn for the next birding adventure.

A day to remember

By Peter Ryan

PART OF THE ALLURE of birding is the uncertainty of the chase. What will I see today? But not all birding outings are stress free; they lie on a continuum from exploratory to targeted. When covering your local patch, you have little expectation that anything exciting will turn up. Such outings typically are enjoyable and relaxing, and give a thrill when something unusual does appear. Twitching lies at the other end of the spectrum. Here, your success rests squarely on seeing a particular bird. The best you can hope for is the satisfaction of finding that bird. Until then, you are plagued by anxiety. And if you dip out, you are left with a depressing sense of despondency. With limited upside and plenty of scope for downside, it's perhaps surprising that ever more people are attracted to the doubtful pleasures of twitching.

Birding in a new area lies somewhere between these extremes. Most birders do their homework before visiting a new area, and have a list of target species they want to see. Although you might not expect to see them all, there are some species you should see, so once again you risk falling into the trap where there is more opportunity for disappointment than elation. When the new area is one with very few species, even more weight is placed on finding the target species. This is a story of searching for a particular bird, where the stakes were especially high, because it is an iconic species that occurs in one of the most hard to get to places on Earth.

The bird in question is the Inaccessible Island Rail – famous for being the smallest flightless bird surviving today. There was a smaller flightless wren in New Zealand, but the last remnants of its population on Steven's Island were hunted to extinction by introduced cats a century ago. As you might expect, the Inaccessible Island Rail is only found on Inaccessible Island, which pretty much sums up your chances of getting there. In fact, the island derives its name from the steep cliffs that back the entire coast, restricting access to a few narrow boulder beaches. However, it is certainly not an easy place to reach.

One of three islands in the Tristan da Cunha archipelago, Inaccessible is the peak of an extinct volcano roughly midway between Cape Town and Buenos Aires. Together with St Helena, Tristan da Cunha forms part of a UK Overseas Territory. The main island of Tristan is home to around 280 Tristanians, who collectively form the most remote permanent human community. Access is only by ship, taking anything from a week to 10 days from Cape Town, the closest port, depending on the weather and the ship's speed.

Once you reach Tristan, it is still a major challenge to get to Inaccessible, some 30 km away. In the 1980s, when this tale took place, the only boats available to make the crossing were used for the lobster fishery at Tristan. They could only venture across the often-treacherous stretch of ocean separating the two islands on good weather days – when typically they would be occupied catching rock lobsters. Only if the good weather day was a Sunday was there a chance of getting a boat to go across. Given that there are only a few good days each month, the chances of getting to Inaccessible were slim at best unless you lived on Tristan.

Such is the remoteness of Inaccessible Island that the first land-based survey only took place in the summer of 1982/83, when Michael Swales led the Denstone College Expedition to the island. In 1956, Swales was the ornithologist on the first scientific survey of Gough Island, another British possession some 380 km south-southeast of the Tristan archipelago. I suspect that he saw an expedition to Inaccessible as a way to re-live his youthful adventures on Gough. With logistical support from the South African Antarctic programme, Swales and his party of mainly schoolboys from Denstone College were landed by helicopter on Inaccessible Island in October 1982. Michael Fraser was appointed expedition ornithologist at the last minute before the team left the UK. On the SA Agulhas en route to Tristan he met birders from the Percy FitzPatrick Institute of African Ornithology, which ultimately led to him registering for an MSc at the Fitz. Mike, and his partner Liz McMahon, are well known for their lovely books on the Cape and its fynbos: *A Fynbos Year*, *Between Two Shores* and *The Smallest Kingdom*.

But I digress. I was an undergraduate student at the time of the Denstone Expedition, completing my BSc in Botany and Zoology. After finishing my honours degree in 1983, I started an MSc on the impacts of plastic ingestion on seabirds – a project that I selected mainly because it entailed visits to Marion and Gough Islands. And so, in October–November 1984, I made my first visit to Gough and Tristan. It was to be the start of a life-long love affair with these magnificent islands. And after spending three weeks on Gough Island, we steamed north overnight to arrive off Tristan at dawn.

We were greeted by White-faced Storm Petrels, dancing in the ship's wake. These longest-legged of storm petrels are strangely hard to see at sea off the islands before their eggs hatch (thereafter you can see them all day long, foraging just beyond the kelp band). But in those days – before the introduced mice on Gough Island took their toll – they were common at night on Gough Island. So I had ticked them at night, but this was my first view of them at sea and in daylight – an auspicious start to what I still regard as the best day in my life. But it all nearly went horribly wrong.

The day was one of those rare clear, calm days at Tristan. As the ship approached the island we could see the island's snow-capped volcanic peak, rising to more than 2000 metres, peeking above the impressive coastal cliffs. And then it was lost to view as we came to anchor off Edinburgh-of-the-Seven-Seas, the grandly named settlement. After an impatient wait for breakfast, it was time to go. John Cooper had arranged for the ship's helicopter to take him, Jim Enticott, Barry Watkins and me to both Nightingale and Inaccessible Islands, to explore for research opportunities at these uninhabited islands. We were to have three hours on each – which should be more than enough time to see the four endemic landbirds: the Tristan Thrush, Tristan and Wilkins' Buntings, and the Inaccessible Island Rail.

After a short flip to shore to collect island guides, we flew to Nightingale Island. En route, we buzzed a small fleet of island longboats, sailing back to Tristan bearing a cargo of 'petrel' (Great Shearwater) eggs. Nightingale is the smallest and oldest of the three main Tristan Islands, and home to a series of huts, where the islanders stay when they visit to collect seabird eggs, chicks and guano. We were dropped on one of the ponds on the island's western plateau. These marshy depressions are filled with dense floating mats of the sedge *Scirpus sulcatus* that more or less support a person's weight – but certainly not the weight of a Puma helicopter. So the chopper hovered, the Atlantic Yellow-nosed Albatrosses clung to their nests, and out we jumped.

A special kind of peace descends when a helicopter departs. You are still on a high from the flight, your ears are ringing from the chopper's cacophony, and then all is calm and quiet. The only sound was the reeling calls of albatrosses, the long-calls of the Subantarctic (Brown) Skuas, and chittering calls from the lush vegetation around the ponds. Lifers! The tiny local form of Tristan Bunting (now split as a separate species, Nightingale Bunting) was common, with pairs chasing around the edges of the pond, and feeding on Scirpus seeds.

Tristan Thrushes or Starchies didn't need searching out – incurably curious, they came to us. First one, then two, and then a host attracted by the querulous, high-pitched *sweep* calls of their kin. These supreme generalists are renowned for eating seabird eggs, and are especially keen to peck at anything rounded, including the toes of wellington boots, the ends of poles, or anything else that stays still long enough to be investigated. In November, their numbers were swelled by broods of recently fledged juveniles, who are even more confiding than their parents, and we were able to take some nice photographs even with only a standard lens.

That just left Wilkins' Bunting, the large-billed sibling of the Tristan Bunting, to locate. They use their large bills to crack open the woody fruits of the Island Tree *Phylica arborea*, the islands' only tree. Interestingly, *Phylica* is a genus centred in the fynbos, where there are more than 200 mostly shrubby species. Tree-like forms have colonised St Helena, Tristan and Gough in the South Atlantic Ocean, and Mauritius, Reunion, Amsterdam and St Paul in the southern Indian Ocean. These giant island forms were once all placed in the same species, but genetic work has shown that there have been at least three colonisation events: one to St Helena, another to Mauritius and Reunion, and a third that first reached Tristan-Gough and then from there all the way east to Amsterdam and St Paul Islands. Such long-distance dispersal almost certainly was mediated by petrels, which retain indigestible prey remains and other debris such as pumice, plastic and woody seeds in their gizzards for months.

But once again I'm deviating from the main storyline. Needless to say, we ventured into the nearest stand of *Phylica* trees and fairly soon located a couple of pairs of these heavy-set buntings by their deeper, slower calls. Recent studies confirm that the large and small-billed buntings on Nightingale Island are each other's closest relatives, and apparently evolved in situ, separate from the radiation of buntings on Inaccessible Island. This makes Wilkins' Bunting one of the world's naturally rarest bird species, with at most a few hundred pairs, limited by the small size of Nightingale Island and the localised distribution of Island Trees. None of these species are buntings in the traditional sense – they are derived from South American tanager finches, and should be called finches rather than buntings.

So, mission accomplished on Nightingale. Inside half an

hour we had seen all three endemics, and were free to enjoy the island and its wildlife without anxiety. That just left the rail to get on Inaccessible.

Our trusty helicopter returned bang on time at 12:00, and whisked us across the 20 km from Nightingale to Inaccessible, where we landed next to the Denstone Hut at Blenden Hall. John was particularly keen to assess the state of the hut, with a view to using it for future fieldwork. This suited the birders among us, because before we left Cape Town, Mike Fraser had told us that the rail was common in the dense tussock grass next to the hut. After a cursory inspection of the hut (which was already showing signs of wear and tear, with a few leaks), we clustered around a marshy area west of the hut and started to search for the rail in earnest.

At around 40 g, the Inaccessible Island Rail is the size of a large mouse, and it behaves in a mouse-like fashion, skulking in dense vegetation to remain secure from the ubiquitous skuas. It is abundant throughout Inaccessible Island; Mike estimated there are at least 5000 pairs. We could hear various high-pitched tip and tip-ip calls, which sounded like Mike's description of its contact calls. And occasionally a trilling song, vaguely reminiscent of that of a Little Grebe, emanated from the depths of the tussock, but the bird itself remained stubbornly invisible. An occasional rustle in the grass would set hearts racing, but invariably turned out to be a thrush.

John was the first to lose patience, and wandered off to explore the other attractions of the island. At the hut, nerves were starting to show. Those favouring a silent 'wait-and-see' approach shot angry glares whenever someone else moved. Various pishing and squeaking calls were tried, but to no avail. Eventually, after we'd spent close to an hour working the best-looking habitat, John returned and started pressuring me to survey the beach for litter – part of my project looking at the abundance of plastic debris on oceanic islands. After some considerable nagging, I reluctantly left for the beach.

My exact feelings at the time are lost to me now. But I have a generic sense of the dread that dipping a particularly important bird can evoke – a sort of gut-wrenching, visceral fear. Fortunately, with age, I have grown out of it to some extent; developed a sense of detachment born perhaps from the perspective of wisdom that comes with experience, or perhaps simply from surviving other such events. But at the time I could only imagine one thing worse than dipping the rail – to be gripped off by the others in the party. And this seemed to be a distinct possibility, given that I was the only one with other work to conduct. Not surprisingly, I had no offers from Barry or Jim to assist with scoring beach litter.

The coast of Inaccessible comprises either sheer cliffs descending directly into the sea, or boulder beaches, mainly made of rocks about 20–100 cm across. Only in a few sheltered bays are there smaller pebbles; any sand-sized particles are swept away by the rough seas. Blenden Hall, named after the British East Indiaman that wrecked there in 1823, lies on the island's western shore. The reef where the ship ran aground shelters a shallow bay, but the rest of the coast is exposed to the westerly winds and seas. I spent the next two hours working systematically along the shoreline from Blenden Hall Bay to West Point, where I found more than 500 litter items in 900 metres of beach. For each I recorded the type of item, its material (plastic, glass, wood, metal, etc.), and searched it for a manufacturer's mark to indicate its country of origin. Unsurprisingly, given the prevailing westerly winds and currents, most of the litter had travelled from South America.

Which is great, but it wasn't getting me any closer to seeing a rail. With time running out, I was resigned to failure, and to find the others basking in the glory of success. Then, with just a few minutes to go before the chopper was due to collect us, I reached down to pick up a piece of litter in a gulley between two large tussock grasses, and there, literally inches from my finger tips, was an Inaccessible Island Rail. Beady red eyes, glossy black bill and fluffy feathers like a kiwi. I froze. It contemplated me for a second or two, and then walked sedately off into the vegetation. Elation! My mood soared, and the day was saved.

I floated back to the hut, where there were vague mutterings of glimpses through the grass. Then the chopper arrived, and we flew back to Tristan, ascending to circle the crater lake on the island's central peak before landing. We rounded off the day doing the tourist round on Tristan, and I even collected some more beach litter from the boulder beach next to the tiny harbour. Three new islands in one day, and all the endemic birds safely in the bag. Life doesn't get any better than that.

Postscript

I assumed that was to be my only chance to see the rail. Yet three years later I was back on Inaccessible Island for several weeks, accompanied once again by Barry Watkins, to measure the rail's metabolic rate. This required catching rails and recording their oxygen consumption overnight, so we got to know them very well. And the following year I started my PhD on the ecology and evolution of the islands' finches. It would have made no difference in the long run whether I saw the rail or not on that first, all-too-brief visit. Yet at the time, had I missed the rail, I would have been gutted, and the day irrevocably tarnished.

Human nature dictates that the harder you have to work

for a bird, the more you appreciate it. I've often heard birders comment how a particular bird would be a real cracker if only it wasn't so common. In the case of the rail, the difficulty of reaching its only home, and then seeing it once you get there (a task made much simpler if you have a recording of its call), certainly adds to its appeal. However, the rail is intrinsically interesting because it is one of the very few flightless rails to have survived the spread of humans and their commensals. Inaccessible and Nightingale are both fortunate to have been spared the scourge of cats, rats and mice.

Since that first visit, I have lived on Inaccessible Island for more than a year. Many of my fondest memories are of days spent fighting through tussock grass, or trekking through the dense fernbush that cloaks the island's plateau. I seldom bother to look for rails any more; usually I encounter them while having lunch, or sitting contemplating the magnificent views. But I still get a thrill every time one pops out of the undergrowth to inspect the lumbering giant who has invaded its island world.

A life going cuckoo

By Claire Spottiswoode

My most powerful memories of childhood all seem to include one thing: eggs. Three bright blue spotted eggs in a tiny nest below a shrieking Levaillant's Cisticola, on the border of a Philippi vegetable field in a Cape Flats spring. Two elongate, olivey eggs felt beneath my finger inside an Orange-breasted Sunbird's nest in, thrillingly, a haze of tubular white *Erica mammosa* flowers below the Kirstenbosch tea-room. A Crowned Plover's lovely mottled egg on my primary school field, not as camouflaged as it ought to have been against the irrigated green grass. (I was convinced that Crowned Plovers must be a rarity, such was their beauty. In the school library, among the gargoyle-like paintings of Hazel Stokes's *Birds of South Africa*, it was a terrible anticlimax to find them described as commonplace on school fields throughout South Africa.) My obsession with birds was aided and abetted by the kind ladies of the Cape Bird Club, who gave me lifts to sewage farms and quarries and saltmarshes, and by my bird hero Peter Steyn who challenged me to a Nest Record Card filling-in contest (amazingly – as it still seems – I won).

But the egg I longed to see above all was the egg of a con-artist. Cuckoos captivated me, but I never found a Diederik Cuckoo's egg perfectly mimicking the technicolour weaver eggs around it, or a Klaas's Cuckoo chick bulging out of a Cape Batis's nest like in Nico Myburgh's carefully gardened photos that I had cut out of calendars and stuck to my bedroom wall, the Prestik leaking into their curling corners. Aged 18 I attended the International Ornithological Congress in Durban as a first-year student volunteer, where I changed the carousels of slides between talks in exchange for a free ticket, my official conference staff shirt drooping down to my knees.

There I had a cuckoo-epiphany. Professor Nick Davies gave a lecture on his research in the unimaginably distant and alien Cambridgeshire fens, and showed us that cuckoos were not just captivating, but they let you actually unpick the process of evolution! I had no idea that you could do simple field experiments to figure out how evolution actually worked, and discover how cuckoos and their hosts were entwined in a never-ending arms race of adaptations for better trickery, and counter-adaptations for better defence. It was sheer wizardry. I was entranced. But I'd still not seen a real live cuckoo's egg.

Nick kindly supervised my PhD and I drove my clapped-out Isuzu around the Kalahari and poked around Sociable Weaver nests. The only nest intruders I found there were Cape Cobras, sometimes tightly coiled in the weaver nest-chambers where they had eaten up my datapoints, at others attempting to slither up my legs and into the observation hole of my shadecloth hide, and most nights infecting my dreams with their coldly terrifying omnipresence. A dead cobra, killed presumably by a honey badger, decomposed to reveal the leg-bones of weaver chicks, still wearing my SAFRING rings and leaving a gap in my experimental spreadsheet.

I was haunted not just by dreams of cobras, but of eggs to the north. Pete Leonard, then an ornithologist-schoolteacher on a farm in southern Zambia, had told me of an egg-collector, Major John Colebrook-Robjent, who farmed tobacco in the miombo woodlands as a means to live in a place full of cuckoos. I had never shared the acquisitiveness of egg-collectors, but totally understood their love for the beauty of eggs. And certainly understood the Major's passion for parasites. I drove my Isuzu to Zambia and was greeted by a man with white hair, piercing blue eyes and a military backbone, standing on the doorstep of a small farmhouse under the *Brachystegia* trees: 'Ah, Spottiswoode of Berwickshire!' The Major's obsession for eggs was equalled only by his passion for British genealogy (in this instance he was to be disappointed). This house was a mausoleum, crammed with meticulously labelled clutches, skins and ledgers of nest records. I spent weeks measuring and weighing and photographing and talking late into the night with the Major, who always dressed for dinner and served bread sauce from a silver pot. We wrote several papers together. In the bright world beyond the sombre farmhouse (kept that way for fear of egg-bleaching sunlight, and mosquitoes), I eventually I found a real cuckoo's egg for myself. Two, in fact, round and turquoise to match the eggs they lay among in an Arrow-marked Babbler's nest concealed in a tangle of thicket. Levaillant's Cuckoo, 20 years overdue. By the time I handed in my Sociable Weaver PhD, my heart was already in the miombo woodlands.

The Major introduced me to Lazaro Hamusikili, his long-standing right-hand man, an ornithological genius, champion nest-finder and tree-climber and egg-blower and skin-preparator. As the Major's health took turns for the worse, Lazaro and his fellow farm-workers started finding eggs for my research instead. Their ability to summon nests out of the tall grass of the Zambian rainy season seemed magical. Cuckoo Finches were my first quarry. Lazaro, Collins, Kiverness, Avedy, Refi, Obvious and many others uncovered hundreds of prinia and cisticola nests every year for me to do my experiments on, as they still do. Prinia eggs were miraculous, every female's egg with its own distinctive signature scribbled across its red, blue, white or green surface – as if to write, *this is my egg* – to foil mimicry by the cuckoo finch in evolutionary hot pursuit. Every four or five prinia's nests contained the astounding eggs of a cheat: one or two Cuckoo Finch eggs, red, blue or white, near-perfect forgeries of their host's signatures – *and so is this*. Every nest felt, and still feels, as thrilling as the ones I found aged nine at Kirstenbosch.

Lazaro mostly laughed and smiled at everything, and even when drunk was still capable of fishing eggs one by one from a Fork-tailed Drongo nest using a little coil of fencing wire attached to the end of a three-metre-long pole. He sways halfway up an *Uapaca* tree, cackling with glee as he finds an African Cuckoo egg among the drongos', balancing its thick bottom on his palm to check its identity before popping it into his mouth for safekeeping as he climbs down.

Honeyguides were next. I started studying them in the dry season of 2008, in the last month of the Major's life. Lazaro hacked through the rock-hard earth – a technique he knew well from hunting rats for relish – to reach bee-eater nests at the ends of the underground tunnels they had dug into the sides of aardvark holes. Every few nests we would find a scene of carnage: bee-eater eggs punctured and festering alongside the gleaming time-bomb laid by the culprit, a female Greater Honeyguide. Sometimes our shaft of light would reveal a honeyguide chick, blind and naked but stabbing, with the pair of needle-sharp hooks at the tips of its bill, at the maimed corpses of the bee-eater hatchlings alongside it; perfectly adapted for siblicide.

In the evenings I reported back to the Major on life and death in his fields, as he lay immobile on a specially welded raised platform in his living room, wracked by spinal TB. He relished every parasitism event. The Major died in November 2008. His widow, Royce, died exactly a year later. In July 2011 Lazaro killed one of his colleagues in my nest-finding gang, Stanley Munkombwe, with an axe, in a dispute precipitated by stolen maize. 'How are the fields, how are the birds?' he asked every time I visited him in jail with supplies of mielie-meal, dried fish and tobacco. He was released in 2014 and to this day, every Zambian spring and summer, continues to find nests, climb trees, and laugh alongside us at the wonder of every cuckoo finch, cuckoo, honeyguide, indigobird or whydah that evolution has allowed to get away with its trickery.

Lazaro also introduced me to the Dr Jekyll side of honeyguides' lives. Every now and then our work would be interrupted by the chattering of a honeyguide with wax, rather than hosts, on its mind. Lazaro would whistle to the bird as we followed it, until he found the bees, lit a fire and, using the same axe he uses to disinter the honeyguide's eggs, opened up the tree cavity and gorged on honey and larvae. Most people in southern Zambia don't share Lazaro's expertise nowadays, and so sadly for us (though not for the bees) honeyguides only rarely enlist our help there.

I was thrilled, therefore, to meet by chance at the bottom of a northern Mozambican mountain, the conservationists Keith and Colleen Begg who live and work in Mozambique's Niassa National Reserve. I learnt from them that in this wonderful wilderness where people and wildlife coexist, honeyguiding is still commonplace: every village has dozens of specialist honey-hunters who cooperate – and, it turns out, communicate – with honeyguides on a daily basis. They kindly welcomed me there, and I am now lucky enough to work alongside another staggeringly skilled group of people who know the bush better than any scientist. Orlando Yassene in Mozambique has taught me as much about honeyguides' lives as cooperative partners of our own species, as Lazaro in Zambia has about their lives as exploiters and executioners of other birds.

The home-made axe continues to be my most valued piece of scientific equipment.

Owls in a cave

By Peter Steyn

As an ardent Strigiphile, a term I coined for a lover of owls, I have been privileged to have observed all of the 12 species that occur in Southern Africa. My studies and photographs are encapsulated in my book *A Delight if Owls* published in 1984 and reprinted in 2009. All my encounters with owls have been memorable, but none more so than those relating to the Cape Eagle-Owl.

This species is elusive and easily overlooked, as I shall recount. It has a discontinuous distribution from sea level in the Western Cape as far north as the highlands of Ethiopia. It is relevant to make brief mention of the three races, or subspecies, of this owl. *Bubo capensis capensis* occurs in South

Africa and, surprisingly, in arid areas of western Namibia almost as far north as the Cunene River. It is only in relatively recent times that it was found in several localities in Namibia, illustrating how easily it may be overlooked. *Bubo capensis mackinderi* is distributed from Zimbabwe northwards to the Kenyan highlands, while *Bubo capensis dillonii* is the Ethiopian race. Of the three *capensis* is the smallest, *mackinderi* very much larger, and *dillonii* is intermediate in size between the two.

So much for the background of Cape Eagle-Owl distribution and my story deals exclusively with *mackinderi*, previously known as Mackinder's Eagle-Owl in Kenya, after Sir Halford Mackinder who made the first ascent of Mount Kenya. Its occurrence in Zimbabwe was unknown until a specimen was collected in the Inyanga highlands in 1967 and then, in 1968, another was recorded in the Matobo Hills well to the south. Subsequently Val Gargett, renowned for her research on Verreaux's (Black) Eagles, found several nests in the hills. It was established that in Zimbabwe the preferred habitat of Cape Eagle-Owls is for bare granite whalebacks or 'dwalas' interspersed with wooded valleys, a factor directly relevant to my retrospective realisation that I had discovered the first nest in Zimbabwe, just a year after it was first recorded at Inyanga!

In June 1968, while I was teaching at Falcon College, situated 56 km south of Bulawayo, I camped at Wabi Hill on Debshan Ranch, Shangani, with members of the school's Natural History Society. The hill is part of an impressive granite inselberg which rises dramatically to a height of 1477 metres from the flat surrounding grassland. We were counting the northernmost population of Cape Vultures which roosted, and very occasionally bred, in eroded hollows on the shady side of Wabi Hill. Once this task was complete, we explored other areas of the extensive inselberg looking for San rock art. During this search we flushed an owl from a cave in a cliff and found a nest with two eggs. The owl disappeared into cover so quickly that we did not get a good view of it and assumed, erroneously, that it was a Spotted Eagle-Owl. However, when Val Gargett subsequently showed me her nests in the Matobo Hills, I realised just how similar they were to the nest site at Shangani.

Fast forward eight years to 1976 when my good friend Dave Tredgold was appointed general manager of Debshan Ranch. While staying with him, I suggested revisiting the cave to see if the owls were still there to confirm my intuition that I had found a Cape Eagle-Owl's nest all those years ago. I described the wooded granite amphitheatre to Dave and on 12 June we set off to relocate the site. On arrival, we climbed up to the cave, and an owl flew out to perch in a tree across the valley. This time I was able to note all the characteristic features of a Cape Eagle-Owl – the orange eyes, rufous plumage, heavy dark blotching on the breast and, especially, the very large feet, enabling it to prey on Jameson's Red Rock Rabbits, their favourite prey, weighing up to two kilograms. The span of the foot is 12 centimetres and this alone is a feature that readily separates it from the smaller Spotted Eagle-Owl.

A shallow scrape at the base of a tussock-like sedge indicated that the owl intended to breed and when we returned a week later there was a fresh egg in the nest. Subsequently a second egg was laid and on 23 July the first egg hatched and the second four days later. The small chicks, with their disproportionately large heads, were rather comical in appearance so we named the larger one Festus and its sibling Gomes, after characters in an American TV series *The Adams Family* currently showing on black-and-white television in Zimbabwe.

When the owlets were eight and four days old, Dave and I erected my portable canvas hide against the side wall of the cave, just two metres from the nest, with a dummy lens and flash heads protruding in front to accustom the owls to the equipment I intended using. We timed our visit for the late afternoon so that, if the female did not return, we could quickly climb up and remove the hide. We hid across the valley with binoculars to watch and our tension was palpable as the sun sank below the horizon – and then she returned! Our gamble had paid off and we waited until well after sunset to confirm that she remained on the nest.

Late the following afternoon Dave installed me in the hide and we double-checked that everything was in place before he left me at 17:30. It was important that I should keep as quiet as possible, so my sandwiches were wrapped in cloth instead of paper and the thermos was carefully placed to avoid knocking it over. As light thickened I heard the distant *wow-wow* call of a Freckled Nightjar while I sat as frozen as the Biblical pillar of salt awaiting the female's return.

She came back soon after Dave left and glared at the hide – her vivid orange eyes felt like laser beams as I held my breath. Then she shuffled forward to brood the chicks and I was able to relax. When could I risk my first exposures? Here was a unique opportunity to take the first pictures of a Cape Eagle-Owl on its nest, but what if she didn't accept the flash going off? Eventually I could wait no longer and at 18:00 I released the shutter. No reaction!

And so began my long night's vigil, making observations and recording them with my camera. It turned out to be an uneventful watch, apart from when, at 19:40, scrunching sounds indicated that she was feeding Festus and Gomes on a small dassie that had been lying at the side of the nest on our arrival. An hour later she again fed the chicks. I was able to observe these and other activities by switching on a torch masked with red cellophane to provide sufficient dim light to illuminate the nest.

It was a very long night, measured out with sandwiches and cups of coffee. My gluteal muscles ached painfully from their long immobility but, eventually, when I had almost dozed off, a series of explosive hoots announced the arrival of the male on the edge of the cave at 05:20. The female left the nest to receive prey from him and he departed after two minutes. He had delivered a male Red-winged Starling, which the female proceeded to pluck, but she did not feed the chicks again. Dave fetched me at 06:30 after my 13 hours in the cave.

On 10 August, when Festus and Gomes were 19 and 15 days old, I spent another 13 hours overnight with the owls. On our arrival two dassies and a young rock rabbit lay beside the nest. The female soon returned and during the night she fed the young on six occasions, but she no longer brooded them. They kept me entertained by walking unsteadily around the nest, flapping their wings and bobbing their heads – delightful behaviour typical of all young owls. They left the nest when they were approximately seven weeks old, but prey remains, including a partially eaten juvenile Lanner Falcon, indicated that they still returned to the cave to be fed.

In addition to my two overnight watches, Dave and I gathered sufficient information on our other visits to make the most detailed contribution on the breeding biology of the Cape Eagle-Owl yet published. Our observations, which included 13 photographs, as well as diagrams and tables, appeared in the June 1977 issue of *Bokmakierie* 29(2): 31–42.

During a lifetime spent studying owls with undiminished enjoyment, nothing quite matched that adrenalin-charged moment when I released the shutter to take the first photograph ever of a Cape Eagle-Owl on its nest in that remote cave in Zimbabwe.

Feathering Memel

By Peter Sullivan

THE KLIP RIVER MEANDERS through 42 bends to arrive in Memel, around sedimentary sandstone and mudstones of shales, winding repeatedly around intrusions of dolerite, part of a succession of rocks formed 300 million years ago in the Karoo Supergroup.

In summer the birds over the river and wetland are beautiful and plentiful, trees green and yellow with pollen, the pervasive aroma of fresh farm pasture with a hint of wetland. The area produces some of the best cattle in the world.

Friends pestered me. 'Next time you go birding, please take us!' Besides wanting to neither publicly display my ignorance nor destroy my unearned and undeserved reputation for knowing my stuff, I don't really like birding with a crowd.

But hey, friends are friends.

So those who had casually asked (and a few who hadn't) were simply informed I'd be going birding in Memel in the Free State for a birding weekend, I'd buy dinner on Saturday night in the small town for those who actually came, and hand out some prizes for beginners on Sunday morning at a brunch when we could share experiences. They were to make their own arrangements for accommodation, the town and surrounds had plenty of places.

I expected about a dozen to pitch up. It was November 1999.

Charlotte of Memel ran a boarding house, and she told me she could easily handle 12 people for dinner on Saturday and then for brunch. We were all set.

When informed that 42 people had accepted, booked and confirmed, I was flabbergasted yet delighted. Charlotte, however, when I arrived at Memel on Friday afternoon after a leisurely three-hour drive from Johannesburg, was in a panic.

'I can't make dinner for 44!' she wailed. 'What will we do? Your friends have booked every single B&B, hotel, house, room and *alles en nog wat* in this town. Jislaaik!'

Yet the same Charlotte suggested a plan. *'n Boer maak mos 'n plan*: oom Frans and tannie Marie had a farm, only 20 minutes from town, perhaps they could do a lamb-on-a-spit braai for all of us on Saturday ...?

Off we trekked to the farm, farmer Frans shook my hand with his massive hands, and quietly agreed to have half a sheep on the spit for us. We would need to bring our own drinks.

Hesitant in his English, relief crossed his rugged face when he heard I was actually a Free State boy and Afrikaans would be fine.

'If you are going birdwatching in the morning, I'm prepared to give you an hour of my time,' he generously offered.

Ungenerously, I refused, not wanting to abuse his hospitality. His face fell. 'I would enjoy it,' he said, earnestly. 'And I know where the birds are.'

'Okay, just bring your bird book and binoculars,' I airily agreed. Puzzlement. He had never heard of a bird book, and did not own binoculars.

At five the next morning we went off birdwatching. With Charlotte he was most enthusiastic, pointing out the birds, and then giving a cry of amazement when identifying them in my book. His face beamed. They did all the work, I simply enjoyed.

Charlotte had arrived with two sets of binoculars, still in their plastic wrap. She apologised, saying she had shown them to the town's dominee, who had sadly told her they were not suitable for birdwatching, but she had brought them anyway in case they could help. They were gifts five years ago from her children. I opened the boxes. They were Pentax and Canon 10x50s, perfect for the job.

Memel is a tiny Free State town that had all the troubles of apartheid's divisions. There was little promise of a future of growth. It is the place the 'rebellie' started. It is said to be where the final shot of the Anglo-Boer War was fired, and General De Wet's son was killed right in front of the NG Kerk that massively ends the main road into town. The Memel Commando was one of the first to take up arms to protest South Africa's involvement in World War One, and 70 men accompanied General Christiaan de Wet in rebelling against the Smuts government. At the age of 11 he had started his military career in doing battle against the Basotho, was first over the top at Majuba, and defeated the English so many times he became a legend. But this is not about him. He was the most romantic of the Boer generals, and he had come to live on a farm near Memel.

These days, residents are largely divided between well-off whites and poverty-cursed blacks. Unemployment is endemic in the township of Zamani, a part of Memel. It is not so noticeable among the white farming community. Worst off of all, according to one township resident, are black farm workers, living on a pittance and having to feed growing families.

There was a glimmer of light. Nature bestowed on Memel the bounty of bird species in their hundreds, supported by a wetland network that is awesome, which is in turn surrounded by beautiful hills, mountains and valleys.

We all had a wonderful braai on the farm on Saturday night, drank a bit too much, and Charlotte managed to cater with tannie Marie's help for the brunch on Sunday morning.

As I had a prize for him, it was disappointing to note Frans was not there. But as I was finishing my little prize giving, he arrived, in dark suit and white tie, fresh from the NG church where he was an officer of the church.

'Oom Frans,' I shouted happily, 'here's your prize of a brand new bird book for having identified the most birds for a beginner!'

He accepted it graciously, but when I boisterously asked in front of all whether he was now a confirmed birdwatcher, he answered ruefully that no, he had consulted the dominee, and had been told it was like gambling, was addictive, and Christians should not do it, although luckily the once he had done it would not count against him as he was not yet addicted.

He received my astounded sympathy.

'But the church council has asked me to ask you to come back to Memel, as we have never had so many visitors, and to tell us what we must do because the town is dying and needs visitors like you.'

Ann Bernstein, founder and CEO of the top think tank

Centre for Development and Enterprise (CDE), agreed to come back with me to talk to the town, and the first date we could find was February 2000.

Ann had been a little bemused that morning because at the place she was staying, the Mooi Pampoen if I recall, two children had woken her early, then stayed at the foot of her bed. Gazing at her. Waiting.

Eventually she asked if they wanted anything, and with big eyes the oldest one wanted to know if it was true that she had killed Jesus Christ? Ann is Jewish. She denied having anything to do with it.

Incidentally, at Christmas that year I received a call from Frans. Excitedly, he told me he was in the Kruger National Park, and had just identified his 100th bird! What about the dominee? 'Ag, to hell with him,' he replied succinctly.

So in February 2000 we had our meeting under a big tree in the middle of town. Due to go from 9 am to noon, then lunch, then leave, it lasted until dark. Everyone was invited. Professor Jeff McCarthy of Durban-Westville's Graduate School of Business ran it for us; he had done the same kind of town hall meetings for virtually the whole coast of South Africa.

Soft spoken, silver haired and absent-minded-professor-like in his thoughtful demeanour, he was the star of the show, drawing thoughts and plans and feelings out of the people present, summarising ramblings crisply before thanking each and every contributor profusely for their excellent contributions.

Secretly I had sent a reporter to the township to encourage the people who lived there to send representatives so we would not have a 'whites-only' meeting, and luckily they did arrive on the morning.

There were a lot of hiccups. The Dominee raised his hand,

and suggested only people who owned property should speak. That was turned down, so he suggested only they should have a vote. Another polite veto from Jeff.

The professor made a long list of suggestions from the floor, and everyone was going to have a vote when the dominee suggested property owners should have two votes. Jeff agreed – saying it would be better if everyone, yes everyone, actually had three votes. On what to prioritise.

At the close of the meeting, Memel agreed on this mission statement:

'Our mission is to realise the world-class birding potential so as to benefit all the people of the Memza area. We aim to enhance people's knowledge of, and access to, our birding environment while ensuring harmony between and within the host community, visitors and our local community.'

They set priorities: Marketing, funding and tourism infrastructure. They elected a committee that had five white and five black people on it, and the chairperson selected was black.

They created sub-priorities to underline their strategies: training entrepreneurs, local management training, learning from other small towns and other birding towns and other tourist destinations so similar mistakes are not made, ensuring local popularisation, creating relationships with provincial, national and international bodies, talking to Rand Water Board, BirdLife SA, and the Audubon Society, putting up signage.

Because it was so late, we were invited into a home to have tea and koeksisters. The new committee was also invited.

The excited lady who invited us also told me very confidentially that it was the first time in her life she had black guests in the room, drinking out of the same teacups.

I found the new chairman in deep discussion with the dominee. South Africa's white heavyweight champion was fighting a black boxer that night, and mischievously I said to the dominee that the new chairman would probably support the black guy.

A while later the dominee pulled me aside, and said he could lay my fears to rest, he had had 'a few words' with the new chairman, and I would be pleased to know he had changed his mind about who he was going to support and would now support 'our man'. Yeah right.

A few months later I wheedled some money from Sasol to get Monty Brett to run a birding course in the town. On the first night Monty called me and said it was hopeless, a total waste of money, the class of about 30 mostly black people just sat, gave no feedback, and had no clue what he was talking about. 'We're just wasting money, I'm wasting my time, I think we should just can it,' he said forlornly.

The next night an overexcited Monty called to say it was the most fantastic course he had ever run. 'They did all their homework, all of it! I couldn't believe it! In Sandton about ten per cent of the people do about ten per cent of the homework, here all 100 per cent did 100 per cent. It is amazing!'

When I returned to Memel to hand over the prizes for the week's course, the 23-year-old new black mayor of the town had come first. Second was Frans, and third was Marie. They were all three beaming such smiles it could have lit up the entire Free State.

Something I still find very moving is that Monty confessed to me that Frans actually won, but had taken him aside and told him to say the Mayor had won, as that would be good for morale. That's real goodness for you.

This all happened in 1999 and 2000.

In January this year of 2017 I was asked to support declaring the whole of the Seekoeivlei wetland reserve a gazetted protected area, instead of just a portion. A splendid idea, being punted by the Free State Provincial Government and supported by BirdLife South Africa.

Much has been done in Memel. The town is not in much better shape, but townsfolk are very aware of the wonderful asset they have and the Free State is doing its best to preserve the area for future generations.

So there's a bird story for you, which does not mention a single bird, but does show that people can be almost as interesting.

My year in miombo

By Warwick Tarboton

I GOT HOOKED ON BIRDS at the age of 11 and by the time I left school at 17 I was a hard-core birder, not in the sense that I had a whacking great life-list, but that birds, and how they went about their daily business, filled most of my daytime thoughts. My parents were of the opinion that I couldn't make a living from this unhealthy obsession so it was decided that the next best thing was for me to become a geologist, where I could at least spend time in the veld. Plans were made accordingly and, to test the water, I secured a job with a geological exploration company in Zimbabwe as a junior field assistant. And so, a few months after leaving school, my miombo adventure started with a two-day train ride from Johannesburg to Harare. I was met there at the station by someone from the Rhodesian Selection Trust Exploration's head office and was shortly thereafter whisked off to the northern part of the country to join and serve two geologists, Jimmy Arnott and Dan Sampey, who were mapping the ancient arkoses that underlay the marvellous woodland around the base camp where we lived, in search of mineralised rock.

Most days I took a gang out to collect soil samples along demarcated grid-lines, me in the lead with a compass, and the team following with a tape, soil auger and sample packets. Our progress was interrupted from time to time when a Greater Honeyguide or when a mixed-species bird party crossed our path. The honeyguide and its insistent calling necessitated someone from the team follow the bird to whichever bee-hive it had in mind, chop the hive open (axe specially brought along for the job) and remove the honey. The mixed-species bird parties, which were mainly a winter phenomenon, gave me my first exposure to miombo birds. These remarkable bird assemblages of ten, 15, occasionally 20 species that spent the day together moving cohesively through the canopy of the trees as they sought insects, included exotic species that I'd only ever seen in books: Spotted Creeper, Mashona Hyliota, Black-eared Canary, White-breasted Cuckooshrike, Retz's Helmetshrike, Cabanis's Bunting and the like.

By the time spring came I'd learnt the calls of all these brilliant new birds and I then started tracking the different pairs down and finding their nests. I focused my activities on a block of woodland next to the camp, my '20-acre area' I called it, and I tried to find every nest of every bird in the block, filling in nest record cards for each and following each nest's progress. Jimmy, who had a camera, came along with me at times but his heart wasn't in it. He did, though, take photographs of some of the nests I found and it included one of me in a tree climbing to a Spotted Creeper nest which CJ Skead used in his book *Sunbirds of Southern Africa* (it appears in the book opposite page 209). And I used more of Jimmy's photos later in an article – my first ever 'proper' publication – which I wrote for *Bokmakierie* on the breeding habits of Retz's Helmetshrike. As my collection of nest record cards grew, I sent copies to the nest record card scheme run by the Rhodesian Ornithological Society (ROS). The organiser was Carl Vernon, a renowned nest finder who befriended me and, probably unbeknown to him, became a role model in how to channel my birding into tackling bird projects systematically.

The late Richard Brooke was, at that time, a leading light in the ROS and he, too, befriended me. He drove up north from Harare one weekend in his little Beetle to meet this loner living in the bush who was sending in interesting records. I'd never encountered anyone like him before, his beard longer than his shorts, and his birding intensity contagious. We subsequently cobbled together an annotated checklist of the birds I'd found in the district which appeared as issue no. 23 of the *South African Avifauna Series*.

Jimmy and Dan left camp every weekend to go to Harare, where they pursued their passion for gliding and so I spent Saturdays and Sundays in camp in glorious solitude, ferreting through the surrounding woodlands like a mongoose. I had another companion from mid-year on until I left Zimbabwe in the form of a Meyer's Parrot. These birds were common in the district and I took him from a nest as an unfeathered chick and hand-reared him. Imprinted as he was, he became another almost human, free-flying member of the camp, making conversation with, and perching on, whoever was around. He joined up with wild parrots from time to time but preferred human company and when I left Zimbabwe he adopted a geologist and his family in another camp.

When I arrived in Harare I'd never driven a car before and, had the company known this, I'd surely not have got the job as the field work necessitated it. So on my first weekend in the bush I was given the keys to a Land Rover and told in no uncertain terms to learn to drive it, with a booking made for a test in the nearest town, Chinoi, the following Monday. The crash course worked and the cursory test saw me qualified to drive forever after. That Land Rover criss-crossed the local countryside, assisted me at times in getting up the bare trunks of larger trees to inspect nests, and from time to time getting irretrievably stuck when crossing the marshy dambos, those wide, shallow drainage lines that form a network of boggy veins criss-crossing the miombo woodland.

Miombo is all but unknown as a veld type in South Africa but from Zimbabwe through to Tanzania and the DRC it extends as a vast swathe of rather uniform broad-leafed woodland best known for its spring colours when the fresh leaves of the msasa and other *Brachystegia* species emerge in crimson glory. It supports a most distinctive bird community and no birding trip to these countries north of South Africa is complete without catching up on the many 'miombo specials'. Sadly, the mature stands of this woodland are much diminished and the loss is continuing apace as population growth in these countries drives the demand for firewood and space for crops. Fifty-something years ago I experienced miombo birding at its best when the woodland and its attendant network of dambos extended from horizon to horizon. Today, viewing the place where I lived and worked and birded through Google Earth, all that is seen there now is a virtually treeless mosaic of cleared lands, huts and footpaths. I wonder whether the people living there today know about honeyguides and their guiding behaviour or even whether honeyguides still exist. Almost certainly, few, if any, of the miombo endemics survive in that depauperate environment.

But it is not only landscapes that have been transformed by the passage of time. Birding too has been transformed and newcomers to this ever more popular recreational pursuit are focused above all on developing their identification skills and networking to find and get to sites where new birds can be spotted. Listing and atlasing are what birding is about today and getting into the hearts and minds of birds and why they do what they do has become largely the domain of academics. For those people who don't get to do post-graduate work in a zoology department or who don't have the budget to dash from rarity to rarity or the health or means to get much further afield than their local patch, old-style birding – making observations and documenting what you see – still offers a supremely satisfying alternative, simply because, given that our knowledge of so many southern African species is rudimentary, new discoveries about our birds lie around every corner. It's the kind of birding that I started out on and it remains part of my psyche today and, to quote someone by the name of Grant Hutchinson, 'There is an unreasonable joy to be had from the observation of small birds going about their bright, oblivious business.'

Goodbye Ghana and thanks for the Gonolek

By Mel Tripp

HAVING BIRDED ETHIOPIA in the north, Tanzania in the east and the southern African countries, Ghana was my first foray into the West African states.

More than any of the other countries in Africa, Ghana left me more polarised with some spectacular highlights and some indelible lowlights.

It was the Cape Bird Club's 2013 International birding adventure.

Dense, damp, and darn difficult ... birding the Upper Guinea Rainforests ... hot and humid too!

This rainforest belt spans much of West Africa, holding some 20 West African endemics, but none unique to Ghana. However, in Ghana, these forests are far more accessible, making many of the special species of these habitats far easier to see than in neighbouring countries ... so we are told.

The other prime habitat was a biome strip of dry Sudan-Guinea Savannah just south of the Sahel in the north of Ghana, virtually on the border with Burkina Faso.

Ashanti African Tours did all our ground arrangements for the trip, including James Ntakor our dedicated bird guide. James is one of three brothers working as bird guides for Ashanti and all three contributed to the 2012 Helm Field Guide, *Birds of Ghana*. Good credentials indeed! Vernon Head (the then chairman of the Club) was our other guide and leader for the trip.

To ease us into the challenging stuff, our first morning was spent in grassland and woodland Savannah of Shai Hills reserve, not far from Accra. Along with some familiar southern African species, we got to grips with the first of many barbets and tinkerbirds. Spectacular and striking species included Splendid Sunbird, whose name has to compete with the Superb and Beautiful Sunbird, which were also seen. I did wonder whether the taxonomist who first described these sunbirds discovered the Beautiful last but had no other superlative better than 'beautiful' left in his lexicon. For to me at least, the 'beautiful' looked more 'superb' and more 'splendid', with its long tail streamers, and more deserving of either of these names.

Then, Violet Turaco ... what a corker, 'cover girl' on the *Birds of Ghana* field guide. Blue-bellied Roller, whose deep purple and azure upper parts contrasting with its white head and breast make it a unique roller. The first of many Western

Grey Plantain-eaters (a turaco), Red-necked Buzzard, a single migratory Whinchat, Vieillot's Black Weaver (one of 12 species of typical weavers we needed to get to grips with) and the tricky (down south) Stone Partridge rounded off a mere stroll in the park compared to what was to come.

A stop at Sakumono Lagoon, en route to our first night's accommodation, was easy wetland birding. However the sight of many Collared (né: Red-winged) Pratincoles roosting among plastic, cans and other debris littering the lagoon was a precedent to much rubbish strewn along the roads in the days to follow.

Kakum National Park was our first upper guinea rain forest experience. A pre-dawn start (aren't they all?) saw us birding the Abrafo forest edge. Screeching overhead had us excited and gazing skywards to see African Grey Parrots flying free in their wild natural state ... a small flock of just four. Sadly apart from one bird towards the end of the trip, this was all we saw of the African Grey Parrot in the wild. In Ghana, the decline in African Grey Parrots has been devastating. It is one of the world's most illegally trafficked birds, now up-listed to 'Endangered' on the 2016 IUCN Red List. A most recent bibliography states: 'Trade and habitat change virtually eliminate the Grey Parrot *Psittacus erithacus* from Ghana' (Annorbah, N.N.D.; Collar, N.J.; Marsden, S.J. 2016. *Ibis* 158: 82–91).

On the edge of some dense forest vegetation James called a halt, indicating for us to listen. From somewhere within we could hear what for all the world sounded like a cheerful artisan going about his business, whistling while he worked. It was mesmerising. We all crept deeper into the damp, dense forest as James tried to lure out this merry soul with a play back. Not a glimpse was had and, frustratingly, in there somewhere, and close, the merry 'human' whistler continued. A Blueshouldered Robin Chat, 'Scarce, irregular and infrequently encountered' says the field guide. So it seemed with all robins, as I for one saw not one single robin on the entire trip! Two spectacular Bee-eaters that day; a Black Bee-eater (voted bird of the day), jet black upper parts contrasting with azure under parts, bright scarlet throat and black and blue streaked breast ... an exquisite small bee-eater. And then the migrant Rosy Bee-eater with its sophisticated slate-grey upper parts, pink under parts, sporting a black mask underscored by a white slash.

Negrofinches, or, if one wishes to be more PC, Nigritas, are odd Estrildids. (The term *negro*, a Portuguese word for 'black' has no racial baggage. Around the 1450s when Portuguese ships entered what is now Senegal, it was dubbed *terra dos negros* (land of the blacks), just an ethnic descriptor, much like Poms or Yanks ... sorry I digress ...) Odd forest-dwelling finches, they do not eat seeds as other finches do but insects! White-breasted Negrofinch was the first of three different species we encountered.

There are 18 species of woodland and forest flycatchers in Ghana. Many of them do their best to impersonate each other ... Ussher's Flycatcher was our first.

Into Abrafo forest again, late one afternoon, with much craning of heads upwards, we encountered Little Greenbul, and the smallest bird in Africa, Tit-hylia ... up in the forest canopy! Why can't it be more obliging and frequent the lower strata? The bird life was not prolific, no doubt due to the background roar of chainsaws assaulting our ears from out in the forest – legal permit logging ... illegal logging? Does it make any difference? Ghana is losing its rain forests at an alarming rate. World Bank figures suggest 80% of Ghana's forests had been destroyed by logging by 2008. One wonders what that figure might be now.

Our third day was full of expectation with a highlight early morning visit to the world famous canopy walkway in the Kakum National Park. Arriving just after first light to make the most of the critical viewing hours and to avoid the 'fun-loving tourists' who treat it as some kind of fairground attraction, we climbed a long series of steep steps to reach the first viewing platform. Strung out through the drifting mist 40 metres up we could see four or five suspended walkways each linked to viewing platforms.

The birding was not what you would call overwhelming. Even James admitted it was 'a bit quiet'. Quiet! I'd say – I only had three new birds on my list after an hour. However, patience, as all birders know, pays dividends and slowly many good birds were seen. Those worthy of mention were our first Malimbe, Red-headed (voted bird of the day), one of four forest weavers, all with distinctive variations of red and black plumage.

That afternoon we elected to visit the Cape Coast Castle, a sobering cultural excursion to one of the 'slave forts' strung along the Gulf of Guinea. Originally built by the Swedes and captured by the British in 1664, from its cramped, dark dungeons and the 'gate of no return' thousands of slaves were shipped to the New World; many never got that far, dying in the appalling dungeon conditions.

In the late afternoon, a dedicated group re-visited the canopy walkway, hoping for some new and nocturnal species. Disappointingly not a lot was seen.

On our last morning in the Kakum forest, the focus was on a secretive and tricky bird. Fortunately this species is terrestrial! James worked hard for this. Finally after many attempts at call-up and almost an hour of peering into dense vegetation, everyone saw the bird ... White Spotted Flufftail (Ghana's only resident flufftail).

After lunch we headed south west to Ghana's only pristine, lowland wet evergreen upper guinea forest, Ankasa Reserve. Almost bordering Côte D'Ivoire, Ankasa protects many of Ghana's specials.

All previous visiting birders had to stay outside the reserve due to there being no serviceable accommodation in the park. Understanding the need to be 'on the spot', Ashanti specially erected tents and installed ablutions adjacent to old ranger's quarters for us... Nice one Mark! (Mark Williams, director of Ashanti.) After three days, two of which experienced torrential rain, it did somewhat take on the appearance of a refugee camp but that all added to the adventure and we were, after all, right in the forest. Owling on two nights produced no owls, a flying squirrel gave us our only nocturnal species. After two days in difficult conditions, the 'roads' were so bad after the rains that even the Land Rovers could not negotiate them, which meant that we had to walk much further than normal to get to some of the prime habitat. One morning (and into the afternoon) we traversed between 12 and 16 km.

The heat and humidity was having strange effects ... directions given, to get onto birds uttered by some ... 'top of that green tree over there!' ... 'on that tree that goes up!'

In spite of this we did see some wonderful birds. At some forest pools, we saw two spectacular kingfishers; White-bellied, Blue-breasted and away from water Chocolate-backed (often heard, but rarely seen). Shining-blue Kingfisher managed to elude us. Bird parties proved to be successful, often orchestrated by Shining Drongos. A Western Bearded Greenbul, with its shaggy yellow beard, inspired a field sketch in my notebook as I sat, in the deepest shade I could find, exhausted from the heat and humidity.

We saw a Fraser's Sunbird; now this is an odd one, a largish, plain green forest sunbird, with a STRAIGHT pale bill! Clearly an evolutionary adaption, as this sunbird is almost exclusively insectivorous.

James made a brave attempt to find White-breasted Guineafowl, a rare Red Data Book species of primary forest. He had seen it here before, earlier in the year. But not this time!

Today the air of excitement was palpable as we headed north to Kumasi, in the central region of the country. In the late afternoon, stopping at the remote village of Bonkro, we disembarked to be greeted by crowds of noisy children and a man in his pyjamas! Samson (the pyjamas are his day wear) has the distinction that 15 years ago he led ornithologists up through the dense forest to a rocky outcrop to discover a bird that for 50 years prior was thought to be extinct in Ghana … the Yellow-headed (or White-necked) Picathartes. After passing through small cocoa plantations, we climbed, single file, up a steep track and then a steep rise to some rocky outcrops to wait quietly below their nesting and roosting caves for this almost mythical, prehistoric-like bird to appear. Suddenly, taking us by surprise after only 14 minutes (Vernon timed it), a ghost out of the forest, one arrived, with agile bounding leaps from branch to rock across our field of view. Awestruck, we sat for a further hour or more as single birds came and went. No one dared move a muscle, not even a camera lens was raised, but I doubt any photo would do justice to what we had just witnessed. Predictably, this was voted Bird of the Trip.

The villagers previously used to harvest the picathartes at their nest sites. Today the tables are turned and income from visiting birders provides far better alternatives to 'roast rockfowl' on the table. Perhaps the income may even extend to some more suitable day wear for Samson?

Walking back, in the forest below, James heard a call he could not identify. Vernon was excited, as he knew that a previous birder to this area had 'seen' Western Wattled Cuckooshrike, an extremely rare species in Ghana, with only two positive sightings. Ours was not to be the third, even after attempts to record the call and play back failed to lure it into view, although we did get a Red-fronted Parrot.

We over-nighted in Kumasi, the bustling capital of the Ashanti region, at the strangely named Royal Basin Hotel. Next morning we undertook the long drive north to the Mole National Park, with the habitat changing through broad-leafed woodland to savannah. En route we stopped for many Grasshopper Buzzards and, now in open country, other raptors included Beaudouin's Snake Eagle, a Red Data Book rare raptor (voted Bird of the Day).

Mole is the largest national park in Ghana, with the Black Volta river away to the west and the White Volta River to the East. The Mole Hotel, in the park, is the only accommodation. As in another place we stayed, TVs in each room are incomprehensively more important than running water! You get used to the 'bucket system' after three days. Thankfully there was air-conditioning, as the heat outside ratcheted up several degrees, but now dry with no humidity. Early morning and late afternoon birding was the order of the days.

Open savannah, woodland, rivers and wetlands provided a good mix of birds ... the list growing rapidly.

Some highlights of note: Around a small river, Pied Flycatcher, Purple Glossy Starling, Yellow-throated Leaflove, Red-shouldered Cuckoo Shrike, Senegal Parrot, and voted Bird of the Day (the spectacularly bright, colourful and exotic ones always are) ... Red-throated Bee-eater. A visit to some dry open grassland yielded Forbes's Plover, a West African endemic (a larger version of our Three-banded Plover), in fact 14 of them, and our only lark of the trip, Sun Lark. What?! ... Did I forget to mention the large, outrageous and stonking Bearded Barbet?!

Oriole Warbler is a largish (20 cm), uncommon warbler, with a distinctive black silvery scaled head and bright yellow under parts and was high on everyone's hit list. After several attempts to locate this bird at various spots, success came for some while crammed into a hide around a waterhole.

An indigobird sighting caused some animated discussion. Of the five species in Ghana, Village Indigobird is the only one easily distinguished in the field – white bill, red legs. All others look very similar to each other and distribution is poorly known. However, a gem of ornithological insight came I think from Simon ... 'You can only positively identify indigobirds by the prey they eat!' ... I think the heat was taking its toll!

We had had little opportunity to do any night birding, until now. So, three nightjars and a Greyish Eagle Owl were most welcome. Long-tailed Nightjar, we had nine on one short stretch of track, easy to ID once you familiarised the gizz. Plain Nightjar, an uncommon migrant, is well ... quite plain. A disappointment, as we were too early, or too late, was no Standard-winged, a spectacular migrant nightjar of these parts. What made up for this was yet to come ... there in the headlights, clearly a different nightjar. Much, much larger than any of the others, with distinctive plumage. James had no clue and no experience of what sat before us. Hastily, most of us thumbing through field guides, Otto slid from the bus, camera ready. Fortunately the bird obliged and several good shots were taken. With this evidence we identified a very rare vagrant to Ghana, just one single red cross on the distribution map ... Red-necked Nightjar! Lifer for all, including our Ghanaian resident bird guide!

Mammals in Mole were disappointingly few. Poaching, bush meat trade possibly?

At Larabanga, a Muslim village just outside the park, we visited what is reputed to be the oldest mosque in West Africa (founded 1421). It is a mud and stick structure of extraordinary architectural design, after the Sudanese style, now restored and well looked after. Standing beside it is a baobab tree and if the legend is true that Ayuba, an Islamic trader who had the dream to build the mosque, is buried beneath the tree, it makes this tree at least 600 years old.

Now, heading further north east, through Bolgatanga and late afternoon, we arrived at the Tongo Hills. In the distance we could see the border of Burkina Faso. The large granite outcrops of Tongo Hills radiated some intense heat, even as the sun dropped westward. One of the local community from somewhere nearby was also over-heated, exchanging angry shouts and abuse at James and Jackson (our assistant guide). Stay calm and keep birding ... some misunderstanding on permission to be there. This was our only disturbing incident on the entire trip. An exception, as Ghana's people are overall affable and friendly. We dipped on one key species here ... Fox Kestrel. Rock-loving Cisticola and Cinnamon-breasted Bunting were seen well. Boarding the bus to head off, a small group of children came bearing an adult bunting and two chicks for sale ... what can one do?

Getting an early start the next morning we headed further north eastwards over the Red Volta River to the banks of the White Volta River, close to the border of Togo, the edge of the Sahel, the dry savannah bordering the Sahara. Stopping on the river edge, Vernon was eagerly first out of the bus, scanning the sandbars ... LIFER! The beautiful Egyptian Plover, a bird he desperately wanted to see. And there two birds patrolled the sandbars, affording us brilliant scoped views of what is the only representative of a new North African bird family *Pluvianus*. This overshadowed Northern Carmine Bee-eaters and African Silverbill, among others.

That afternoon a foray to Tono Dam produced Chestnut-bellied Starling, another special of the region.

Veils of smoke hung in the air from grass fires, pre-empting the Harmattan trade winds that bring sand and dust from the Sahara all the way down to the Gulf of Guinea, blocking the sun for days on end. Time we were heading back south...

On our penultimate day we had a marathon drive south, back to Kumasi. On the way up we had tried unsuccessfully, due to impassable boggy tracks, to get into the Offinso Forest Reserve, one of the few locations for another special and quite rare bee-eater. James was determined to try again. Coming up the now passable roads in the forest we encountered huge logging trucks hauling out sections of what were very old, large rain forest trees. We were reprimanded by the loggers for attempting to take photos. More sobering reminders of the destruction of Ghana's rain forests.

In a clearing, at the intersection of two logging roads, near an abandoned excavator, James, or was it Franz, had seen a small bee-eater. All binoculars were trained on an opening between the trees. Yes ... sure enough, not one, but two Blue-headed Bee-eaters, flitting back and forth hawking insects. Deep purplish blue with rich chestnut back and small scarlet throat patch ... What a corker! But how long will they survive here?

Our final birding en route to Accra was into Bobiri Forest Reserve, a lovely butterfly reserve. We encountered four hornbill species, including two new ones; Black Dwarf and Red-billed Dwarf Hornbills. Finsch's Flycatcher Thrush and Black-winged Oriole were also new birds, plus another sighting, a single African Grey Parrot, this time good enough for photos. Lunch, a clean-up and shower on site and we headed for Accra.

Ribbon development: the expanding and ever growing population spreads along every stretch of arterial road, with shacks, homes and traders. Charcoal is the main fuel for cooking in Ghana. Huge trucks piled high with bags of charcoal, depots and sellers were all along this route to supply Accra. One wonders just how long the forests and the trees will sustain Ghana's burgeoning population.

Bush meat trade was also prevalent on this stretch of road. Mostly 'spatch-cooked' rodents and birds but to everyone's horror, one man offered a live Tree Pangolin held up by the tail. Needless to say this did not go onto the mammal checklist.

At dusk, as we drove to Kotoka airport, through the congested, noisy and frantic Accra traffic, flocks of something were flying out above. Wave after wave of Straw-coloured Fruit Bats ... thousands of them that apparently roost in a few trees at a military hospital in town. It was a spectacular sight and perhaps a fitting symbol that no matter what human-induced challenges, set-backs and destruction, nature will survive.

Oh yes ... the Gonolek?

A beautiful bush shrike, in the boubou family... The Yellow-crowned Gonolek was seen on several occasions by everyone, but me! Stopping at a lake en route north to Tongo Hills the cry went up 'Mel! Mel!' ... Gonolek! A pair and brilliant views too – Thanks James, thanks Ashanti. Thanks Ghana and goodbye!

Extracted and rewritten from a full trip report first published in Promerops Part 1 March 2014 No.297, Part 2 June 2014 No.298

It was a dark and stormy night ...

By Mel Tripp

It was a dark and stormy night ... I once read that this was one of the 'best first lines to start a story' but then again I also recall it being described as 'the literary poster-child for bad story starters'.

Well, it was dark and it was night time but we had dodged the monsoon season.

It was Sri Lanka. It was the Cape Bird Club 2015 International birding adventure.

On our third day we were deep into evergreen rainforest, the Kitulgala Forest Reserve. Dense rain forest is never easy birding, particularly canopy-dwelling species, the use of 'green laser pointers' has become an invaluable tool to get people onto birds and has been embraced by bird guides across the world.

We had picked up some good forest specials, tricky endemics like Legge's Flowerpecker, Spot-winged Thrush, Chestnut-backed Owlet, Layard's Parakeet. Our local bird guide Chaminda, PR Chaminda Dilruk to give him his full title, was proving his worth as one of the country's top birders. Little did we know right then just how good he would be.

We trekked deeper into the forest, across streams, through tangled undergrowth, up embankments, down valleys, then Chaminda was gone. Twenty minutes later he returned. Asking for absolute silence, he beckoned us to follow. In single file we ascended a steep incline along a narrow track. Then he ordered us to stop and wait. Again absolute silence was called for. One by one, crouching low we each followed Chaminda further. He raised his hand, not a word was spoken, indicating ahead with a concealed pointing finger, a few metres off the ground ... leaves! I could see leaves. Bringing my bins up, I focused to where now a small bright green spot was hovering.

Oh my word, above the green laser spot sat an owl, no bigger than the leaves, eyes closed to slits, beautifully camouflaged.

This was it! *Otus thilohoffmanni* ... Serendib Scops Owl. Only discovered and described as a new species for Sri Lanka in 2001. Birders know well that controlled level of contained excitement on seeing birds such as this. The heart races, the blood pumps faster, the neurons in the brain fire a 21-gun salute. I wasn't even steady, crouched on my haunches and in danger of toppling over, such was the excitement.

Everyone in the party was treated to this, one by one taken to the prime viewing spot and returned with smiles on their faces as big as ... well you can think of an adjective!

Back to the main story ... the dark and the night time bit ...

This deserved a celebration, a toast. The place we were staying only served beer. We wanted wine, good wine, South African wine, although this seemed an unlikely prospect.

Bandara, our driver, said he knew a place. A few of us jumped into the bus and off into the night. A short ride into the darkened streets and there, sure enough, dimly lit, a bottle store. LIQUOR WIN & BEER the sign read in English. The beautiful soft and rounded characters of the Sinhalese looked far more elegant and no doubt spelt correctly. Some characters in their softly rounded alphabet have a striking resemblance to a fine fulsome bosom or even a cheeky backside, these always seemed to stand out to me.

We were also fortunate that the moon was not full that night. Poya, which falls about every 30 days and follows the lunar calendar, are religious holidays. If there's a full moon, the sale of alcohol is forbidden ... anywhere.

Now, imagine a shop front, no door, glassed windows, heavily steel grated and barred with just a small opening, just large enough to pass bottles out and money in. 'This place won't sell decent wine,' I exclaimed to Sam ... (Ah did I forget to mention the affable and brilliant Sam Woods, Tropical Birding bird guide? We had arranged the Sri Lanka trip through Tropical Birding, after Sam had led us on a wonderful Ecuador adventure in 2012.)

Vernon then noticed a few bottles of wine displayed in a side window, among the array of spirits, mostly half-jacks and rows of Cinzano (are there people who still drink Cinzano?). Peering at the wine the labels suggested Australian. A Serendib Scops Owl deserves better than Australian!

Then another call from Vernon: 'They have more on the top shelf at the back of the shop'. But with no door, no entrance, how on earth is one supposed to see what's on sale?

'n Birder maak 'n plan. 'Sammy, lend me your bins ...'

I said he was brilliant, a good birder never goes anywhere without binoculars, even to buy wine at night! I raised the bins to scan the back shelves. 'Looks like more Australian, I can see Tall Horse and there is some French wine.'

'French, French ... yes we must have French. A beautiful Bordeaux or Burgundy, it must be red,' exclaimed Vernon.

'I can see a Côte du something, a Châteaux something ... but I'm not familiar with French wines, I really don't know.'

Vernon now took over the bins, clearly an aficionado of French wine. 'We will have the Grand Vin de Bordeaux,' he pronounced with grand aplomb ... 'How many bottles?'

Bandara now spoke in Sinhala to the man at the counter. Our noses pressed to the window, fingers pointing to the top shelf, we tried to get him onto the Grand Vin. Vernon still had the bins, 'more left, more left', of course he didn't understand a word. Bandara translated but without success.

'Sammy, use your laser pointer!' I exclaimed. The bright green spot hovered ... up, up, left, left ... 'there, right there!'

We all collapsed with hysterical laughter, Sammy with tears in his eyes, barely able to talk, cried (literally) ... 'You couldn't make that up!'

Only birders could do that.

Birders, don't ya love 'em?

Riding the rainbow into paradise

By Ross Wanless

I KNEW THERE WAS PROBABLY going to be trouble. So I got to Nelson Mandela International Airport, in Cape Verde, with more than two hours to spare. I didn't really have a plan, except to hope for the best. Sao Tome and Principe (STP) is a tiny country of two islands and scattered islets, rich in endemic birds – like Giant Sunbird, Dwarf Olive Ibis, and the near-mythical Grosbeak, which my friend Martim Melo had rediscovered a few years earlier. I'd heard about these islands in 1993, and it was now 21 years later, and my chance to get there – an ambition that I'd harboured more-or-less since I started birding – was in serious jeopardy.

I'd been planning the trip for more than a year, joining an expedition to census the seabirds at the only remaining seabird colony of any significance in the entire Gulf of Guinea. That was the official reason, and the money behind how I was getting there. And there were two colleagues waiting for me, neither of whom had done much seabird counting, so I was an integral member of the team. But it was the birding on the side – on both islands – that I was really most gutted about possibly missing. The problem was I was stuck in Cape Verde, trying to catch an Air Angola flight to the islands. But STP had recently ventured into the digital world and had an online visa application process that still had a few teething problems. And I was receiving one of those problems. I'd applied well in advance, and then put it out of my mind until shortly before arriving in Cape Verde. In the day and a half I had spent in Praia, over a weekend and without internet access, I'd begun to fret, because the email confirming my visa application hadn't arrived, and there was now no way I could chase it up. My flight was leaving just before midnight on Sunday, so I arrived at 21:30, to give me some time in case negotiations were required. Would I make it onto the flight? Had my visa been granted?

I stood in the queue at check-in. The lady at the counter took my passport and flipped through it once, twice, and then more carefully a third time. Not good. 'Onda estas tu visto?' she asked in Portuguese. I answered in my rudimentary Portuñol, and rather optimistically, 'It's an electronic visa – there's nothing in my passport.' She turned and beckoned to the flight controller, who promptly came over. I broke into a sweat and the butterflies in my stomach started up with intent. I explained to him, and he didn't buy it for one second. 'I need to see your visa – do you have an email?' he asked.

'Well,' I said, bluffing madly, 'do you have internet access, I haven't checked mail for a few days so it's probably there, but on gmail so I cannot find it without internet access.'

'Sure, there's free wifi here.' He didn't flinch, and certainly was not hedging for a bribe, which I wouldn't have paid anyway.

'Okay,' I said, 'I'll check.' My mind was racing, my heart thumping, and I knew this was the moment of truth as a plan hatched in my mind, instantly, fully formed and ready to be implemented. 'What, exactly, do you need to see in the visa confirmation email?' I asked him.

'A reference number,' was his simple response.

I dragged my bags over to a vacant counter, hauled out the laptop and fired it up. First – check gmail – no visa. No surprises there. So I kicked in the plan and created a new email account – VistosSMF@gmail.com. I then went to the Vistos SMF site, the one which had failed to send me my visa, and downloaded the company banner, which was, conveniently, a jpeg. Next – google translate. And I proceeded to translate into Portuguese notification that my visa had been issued. I used short phrases, to ensure that I didn't make egregious errors, for my basic knowledge of Portuguese grammar was no match and I couldn't afford to be tripped up. I made credible (to me) looking text, pasted it into the email, dropped in the jpeg banner, and typed in: Numero de referencia: 12867jho22h. That done, I emailed it to myself, and then logged back into gmail. And lo and behold, there was the email from VistosSMF@gmail.com!

I didn't have to feign relief when I called the controller over and pointed to the screen. He peered at it, turned and looked at me, and then, quite miraculously, he asked me, pointing to the reference number: 'is this the reference number?'

I shrugged and put on my most innocent look: 'Well, it says "Reference number", so yes, I guess it is.'

'Okay,' he said, and indicated to the check-in attendant that she could clear me for boarding. I couldn't believe it. The ruse had worked. At least, it had worked inasmuch as I was now able to get onto the flight to STP. But what would happen when I landed?

It was the most angst-ridden, wretched six hours of my life. I couldn't sleep, fretting over what might happen when I landed, and if my visa hadn't been granted. As we were approaching the island, I drank in every second of morning light and greenery on offer, in case that was all I would see of it. A rainbow appeared briefly – a sign that my father would instantly have recognised as being from God. I was less convinced, but happy to take whatever good omens were on offer – the rainbow is an optical illusion of sorts, there but not really there, a trick of the light. Was I riding in on a rainbow? Or was I kidding myself?

I tried desperately to identify any birds through the window of the plane as we taxied to the terminal – I might at least walk away with one or two lifers! Alas, nothing I could actually tick. I dawdled in getting off the plane, ensuring I was last in the passport queue so that I could sum things up and prepare myself, if possible, for what may come. Knees shaking and nervous sweat once again breaking out, this time disguised under the tropical heat of the island, I handed my passport to the lady at the passport control. She took it, glanced at her computer screen and informed me that I needed to pay the visa fee at the next counter.

And that was it. I was in! My visa had, in fact, been granted, and I later discovered it was in the spam folder, waiting there all along. The trip was more eventful, but nothing approaching the excitement I'd experienced in getting there. My time at the Tinhosas islands was unforgettable, and my colleagues and I succeeded in getting the expedition written up and published, making it the first peer-reviewed paper on the island's seabirds for about 30 years. I didn't see all the endemics on either island, so I shall have to return to those magical isles. But not without a visa in the bag!

Contributors

David Allan

David Allan has been the Curator of Birds at the Durban Natural Science Museum for the past 20 years. Prior to this he worked at the University of Cape Town for nearly a decade at both the FitzPatrick Institute and the Avian Demography Unit (ADU). At the FitzPatrick Institute he studied bustards and cranes in the Karoo and Western Cape regions and this work culminated in an MSc degree. At the ADU he was primarily involved with the Southern African Bird Atlas Project but also contributed to several other ADU projects concerned with road counts, waterbird surveys, the nest record card scheme and the Important Bird Areas project. David started his career in ornithology with the erstwhile 'Transvaal' provincial natural conservation authority where he worked for Dr Warwick Tarboton for several years, mainly on surveys of birds of prey and of rare and threatened Highveld birds.

Mark D. Anderson

Mark Anderson has studied aardwolves, termites, Ludwig's Bustards, Blue Cranes, waterbirds, flamingos, vultures and raptors. For about 20 years he worked in the arid Northern Cape, an area he got to know intimately. Since 1998 he has been employed as Chief Executive Officer of BirdLife South Africa, one of Africa's foremost conservation NGOs. Mark is a passionate conservationist, naturalist and wildlife photographer. His favourite times are spent with his wife, Tania, aimless walking in the bush, watching and photographing all things wild. He has dedicated his life to the conservation of South Africa's natural environment.

Mark Brown

Mark heads up the Nature's Valley Trust, an award-winning community-driven conservation NGO in the Garden Route, working on sustainable solutions to everyday conservation problems. An NRF-rated scientist, and affiliated to the University of KwaZulu-Natal, Mark's focus is on investigating the effects people have on biodiversity, how to mitigate it, and how to engage people in a positive way on these issues.

Callan Cohen

Callan is inspired by sharing the birds and natural history of Africa's wild places with others. He has led over 150 tours and expeditions to 23 African countries for Birding Africa, a bird tour company he founded in 1997. Callan has co-authored two birding books and publishes his research as an associate of the FitzPatrick Institute of African Ornithology at the University of Cape Town.

Susie Cunningham

Susie grew up in New Zealand and obtained her BSc in Ecology & Biodiversity from Victoria University of Wellington. She completed her honours and PhD at Massey University in the Manawatu, working initially on the foraging behaviour of kiwi, and expanding her research into non-visual senses used by probing birds, including kiwi (Apterygidae), ibises (Threskiornithidae) and shorebirds (Scolopacidae). Susie discovered that a unique anatomy and associated vibro-tactile sense thought only to exist in shorebirds has also evolved in kiwi and ibises – suggesting a beautiful case of convergent or parallel evolution. Susie's PhD was awarded in 2011.

Susie accepted a post-doctoral fellowship at the Fitztitute in 2010 to work on the 'Hot Birds' desert birds and climate change programme, in conjunction with Prof. Phil Hockey and core Centre of Excellence team member Prof. Andrew McKechnie (University of Pretoria). Following Phil's sad and untimely passing in 2013, Susie accepted an extension to her fellowship to continue managing the University of Cape Town branch of 'Hot Birds' in collaboration with Prof. McKechnie.

Susie was appointed to the post of lecturer in 2015 and is continuing the 'Hot Birds' programme as well as coordinating the Fitz's Conservation Biology Masters course.

W. Richard J. Dean

W.R.J. (Richard) Dean (M Sc, Botany, Ph D, Zoology), has been a full-time biologist since 1972, initially working in the field in Angola, Namibia, Zimbabwe and South Africa. From 1974 to 1978, he was a research assistant at Barberspan Ornithological Research Station, and from 1979 to 1982 was the Officer-in-Charge of Nylsvley Nature Reserve. In 1982 he was elected an Associate Member of the Transvaal Museum, and in 1995 an invited Guest Scientist at the UFZ-Centre for Environmental Research in Leipzig, Germany. He was awarded the Gill Memorial Medal in 2009 for his lifetime contribution to the knowledge of southern African birds.

From July 1986 to his retirement from academia at the end of 2006, Richard Dean had been a Research Officer at the Percy FitzPatrick Institute of African Ornithology, studying plant–animal interactions and the biology of birds in arid and semi-arid ecosystems. Recent projects include books, *The Birds of Angola* and *Nomadic Desert Birds* and editing (with Sue Milton) a synthesis of research in the Karoo.

Morné du Plessis

Morné du Plessis is passionate about seeking ways in which nature and people can co-exist and thrive.

Dr du Plessis was appointed as CEO of WWF South Africa

on 1 September 2007. Previously he was the Director of the Percy FitzPatrick Institute (PFIAO) at UCT for 11 years. He served as the Assistant Director of Biodiversity Research at the former Natal Parks Board and spent two years as a postdoctoral associate at the University of California at Berkeley.

He holds a BSc Agric (Stellenbosch), BSc Hons (Pretoria), PhD (Cape Town) and an MBA (Cape Town).

Vernon RL Head

Vernon RL Head was born in 1967 in a bungalow near the sea and the gulls. He studied architecture, winning national and international awards for design and creative thinking. When not designing strange buildings, he spends his time travelling the world looking for rare birds. He is a poet and author. His first book, *The Search for the Rarest Bird in the World*, became a bestseller, was published internationally, and achieved critical acclaim; it was long-listed for the Alan Paton Literature Prize. Athol Fugard described the work as 'truly enthralling', the *Wall Street Journal* described it as 'all-consuming, panoramic, exquisite ... and a Nabokovian ride'. He is past chairman of BirdLife South Africa and presently serves on the Advisory Board of the FitzPatrick Institute of African Ornithology at the University of Cape Town.

Alan Kemp

Alan was born and bred in Zimbabwe, attending a high school in the bush where natural history was encouraged and offering his collecting, egging, nesting, falconry and hunting skills to

Dr Bob Brain of the National Museums in his holidays. He graduated with majors in Zoology and Entomology from Rhodes University, where vacation work under Gordon Maclean in the Kalahari led to his first job studying raptors in Kruger Park as research assistant to an American university. While there he began his lifelong interest in hornbills, starting with a PhD on the small species and then, after appointment as an ornithologist under Dr Brain at the Transvaal (now Ditsong) Museum in Pretoria, extending this to a long-term study of the ground hornbill in Kruger and then to other species (and raptors) elsewhere in Africa and Asia. He met his wife Meg at Rhodes, they married a year after graduation, worked together formally for a decade at the Transvaal Museum, and then informally, together with their daughter and son, so far for the rest of their lives.

David Letsoalo

David Letsoalo has been described as one of the top birding guides in South Africa by those in the know and was awarded BirdLife South Africa's Eagle Award in 2007 for being the Top Local Bird Guide in South Africa – the only person to ever win this title. Apart from his sound birding expertise, he has sharp eyes and ears essential for the often frustrating forest birding experience. The reason why a birding outing with David is magic, however, is because of his infectious enthusiasm. When he sees a Black-fronted Bush Shrike for the hundred and second time, he is just as excited as the first time. He patiently explains its position until everyone in the group has found it and then gives in to excited comments – 'it is so beautiful, wow, can everyone see it?' David changes his pace and his level of information depending on whether he is guiding a twitcher or a beginner, a hiker or a slow-pacer. He also shows his interest and enthusiasm about everything the group is seeing, be it a huge tree, a mushroom or a butterfly.

Rob Little

Rob was born in Durban, KwaZulu-Natal, attended school at King Edward VII High School and his conservation career began as a forester in 1974. He attained national diplomas in Forestry and Nature Conservation, a BSc degree in Wildlife Resources from the University of Idaho, USA, and a PhD degree on the behavioural ecology, management and utilisation of the Grey-winged Francolin from the University of Cape Town. During 1974–1985, he was a forestry researcher, lecturer in forestry and nature conservation and warden of the Cathedral Peak mountain catchment reserve in the KwaZulu-Natal Drakensberg. During 1988–1997, Rob coordinated the Gamebird Research Programme at the FitzPatrick Institute of African Ornithology, University of Cape Town. Rob was Director: Conservation at WWF South Africa during 1997–2008. In April 2009 he was appointed Manager of the Centre of Excellence (CoE) at the Fitztitute. He is the Fitztitute's link with the National Research Foundation and the Department of Science & Technology and manages the research activities that are funded by the CoE using Birds as Keys to Biodiversity Conservation.

Rob has authored over 80 papers in peer-reviewed journals, including book reviews, over 100 semi-popular articles, four books and seven book chapters, including 14 species accounts in *The Atlas of Southern African Birds* (Vol. 1, 1997), 12 species accounts in *Roberts' Birds of Southern Africa* (Vol. VII, 2005), and 25 species texts in *The Ultimate Companion for Birding in Southern Africa* (Vol. 1, 2014). Together with Tim Crowe, he published the book *Gamebirds of Southern Africa* in 2000 (second edition 2011), and in 2016 he published the *Terrestrial Gamebirds & Snipes of Africa* with Jacana Media. Rob is an Associate Editor for the journal *Ostrich*, and guest edited a special issue of *Ostrich* in 2015 (Vol. 86(1&2) in memory of Phil Hockey, which attracted 20 papers, 17 with Fitztitute authors and 12 with Phil as co-author.

John Maytham

John Maythem is host of the Afternoon Drive Show on CapeTalk and a passionate lover of birds.

Adam Riley

Adam Riley has grown up with a lifelong interest in wildlife, which evolved into a particular fascination with the birds and mammals of the world. Coming from a rural background in KZN, he studied accountancy and qualified as a Chartered Accountant after doing articles with KPMG in Pietermaritzburg. However Adam decided to pursue his passions and has since founded several ecotourism companies including Rockjumper Birding Tours, Rockjumper Wildlife Safaris and ORYX Photographic Expeditions. Adam has as a result travelled extensively, leading tours to numerous destinations ranging from Antarctica to Alaska, Angola to Guyana and Bhutan to Papua New Guinea. Adam is one of Africa's most experienced birders, having seen over 2000 species on the continent and over 8000 worldwide, many of which he has photographed. Adam lives in Hilton with his wife Felicity and two sons William and Alex.

Peter Ryan

Peter Ryan was born in Yorkshire, UK, but moved to Cape Town at age 10. He was schooled in Fish Hoek before completing his undergraduate training in Botany and Zoology at UCT. Having had a long-standing interest in birds, he joined the FitzPatrick Institute of African Ornithology to study the impact of plastic ingestion on seabirds for his master's degree, and then completed his doctoral studies on the radiation of finches in the Tristan da Cunha archipelago. Peter taught ornithology at the University of California, Davis before returning to UCT in 1993 to coordinate the Fitztitutes's master's programme in conservation biology, a role he continued until he took over as Director of the Fitztitute in 2013. Peter works on a variety of topics, but seabirds and their conservation are his main focus. He has published more than 300 peer-reviewed papers, 12 books and 200 popular articles.

Claire Spottiswoode

Claire Spottiswoode is a birdwatcher and biologist. She works jointly in South Africa and the UK, at the FitzPatrick Institute of African Ornithology at the University of Cape Town, and in the Department of Zoology at the University of Cambridge. Her research mainly involves coevolutionary interactions between species, such as parasitism and mutualism, and African conservation biology, all inspired by life-long birding in southern and eastern Africa. With Callan Cohen and others, she has written three birding guidebooks to southern Africa and Ethiopia. She lives in Scarborough on the Cape Peninsula and in a village in the Cambridgeshire fens, and is married to another birdwatcher, Tim Dee.

Peter Steyn

Peter Steyn has been passionate about birds from an early age. Born and educated in Cape Town, he moved north on completion of his degree to teach in Zimbabwe. He 'retired' from schoolmastering at the age of 34 to devote all his time to ornithological research, wildlife photography and writing books.

After 17 years in Zimbabwe, he returned to Cape Town to new horizons. As a freelance specialist bird guide, he has travelled throughout Southern Africa, especially to Botswana, and has lectured on expedition cruise ships from the Arctic to Antarctica.

His published research, especially on birds of prey, has been widely acclaimed. In 2011 he was awarded the prestigious Gill Memorial Medal 'for an outstanding lifetime contribution to the knowledge of Southern African birds' and in 2012 he received the Steven Piper Lifetime Achievement Award for his contribution to raptor conservation and research.

His ten books include *Eagle Days, Birds of Prey of Southern Africa, A Delight of Owls, Hunters of the African Sky, Nesting Birds* and *Antarctic Impressions.* His memoir of 70 years of birdwatching is encapsulated in his latest book *Kingdom of Daylight – Memories of a Birdwatcher*, published in 2017.

Peter Sullivan

Peter Sullivan is a political journalist, was editor of *The Star*, is a former Chairman of BirdLife South Africa, has sailed across two oceans, visited 68 countries and is a proud Free Stater – and tenth generation South African.

Warwick Tarboton

Warwick Tarboton grew up in Johannesburg and began life as a geologist but changed tracks a few years later to pursue a career in ornithology. Initially he worked (for 20 years) as ornithologist in the Directorate of Nature Conservation in the former Transvaal Provincial Administration and thereafter he freelanced, writing about, consulting on, and photographing birds and, more recently, on dragonflies too. He has contributed extensively to the bird literature in South Africa and has authored or co-authored a number of books. He lives with his wife Michéle outside Modimolle in Limpopo province.

Mel Tripp

Mel Tripp is a Post WW2 baby, born in Chiswick, London. He cut ties to home at 26 years of age and, after several journeys around Europe, headed to the New World. He travelled the Americas; North, Central and South for almost a year. In December 1972, he landed in Johannesburg from Rio de Janeiro, and was almost immediately deported, but that's another story.

In 1973, Mel worked for a safari company guiding trips to Botswana and Rhodesia (it was called that then) and this kick-started his interest in birds in Africa.

After that he spent six years in Durban building a yacht, but didn't get to sail the big blue.

He moved to Cape Town, where his passion for birds took off, when he joined the Cape Bird Club circa 1982. He held the position of vice chairman of the Club for six years and chaired their 50th and 60th Jubilee celebration sub committees. Many International birding trips followed, as well as much birding in southern Africa.

In between all this, he pursued his career in the advertising world, working as a creative at many top ad agencies. This was followed as a lecturer at the AAA School of Advertising in Cape Town and subsequently as the campus administrator for over 10 years. During this time he became involved in voluntary marketing work with BirdLife South Africa.

Now retired, Mel is currently sitting on BirdLife South Africa's marketing committee, as senior marketing advisor.

Ross Wanless

In 2007 Ross completed his doctoral thesis, which was awarded Best Doctoral Thesis in the Science Faculty at the University of Cape Town, and which took third place in the United Nations/Convention on Migratory Species international thesis competition. Ross joined BirdLife in 2008, taking up the position of Africa Coordinator for the BirdLife International Marine Programme.

He leads BirdLife South Africa's seabird team, including the acclaimed Albatross Task Force. In 2012 at the IOTC

Commission meeting, he helped broker an agreement between fishing nations to use Best Practice recommendations to reduce seabird bycatch in tuna longline fishing and in 2013 the Republic of Korea invited Ross to lead the collaborative research onboard their high seas bluefin tuna longline fleet.

After the first World Seabird Conference (2010, in Canada), he revived the African Seabird Group. He then led a successful bid to have Cape Town host the second international World Seabird Conference, in 2015, chairing the local organising committee. Ross is now on the Executive Committees of the WSU and the Pacific Seabird Group.

Ross oversees two BirdLife staff in West Africa. He has also launched ambitious new conservation programmes. One of those is to halt the catastrophic collapse of African Penguin numbers in South Africa. Another is to have mice eradicated from South Africa's Marion Island, in the southern Indian Ocean.